Taste of Blackville

A collection of recipes from
Calvary Fellowship Mennonite Church

© Copyright 2013 Calvary Fellowship Mennonite Church
All rights reserved. No part of this publication may be
reproduced, stored in a retrieval system or transmitted,
in any form, or by any means, electronic, mechanical,
photocopying, recording, or otherwise, without the prior
permission of the publishers.

For additional copies contact your local bookstore or:
Calvary Fellowship Mennonite Church
2954 Healing Springs Road
Blackville, SC 29817
803-284-5006
tasteofblackville@gmail.com

Proceeds from this cookbook will be used to support our
Christian day school. (See photo on back cover.)

Design & Layout | Maria Yoder and Deborah Shank

Carlisle Printing
OF WALNUT CREEK LTD

2673 Township Road 421
Sugarcreek, OH 44681

A Note of Thanks

Thank you to the ladies who shared their recipes for this project!

It took many other hands to bring this cookbook to a reality - Shank's Photo for the photographs used throughout the book on the category divider pages, and the graphic design folks at Carlisle Printing!

Thanks to each of you.

Table of Contents

Appetizers, Dips, Beverages 1

Breads, Breakfasts. 21

Salads, Dressings 53

Soups, Sandwiches 69

Meats, Main Dishes. 83

Vegetables, Sides 119

Cakes, Cheesecakes, Frostings 133

Cookies, Bars, Candies 147

Desserts. 171

Pies. 185

Canning, Freezing. 195

Miscellaneous 205

Index. 215

Appetizers, Dips, Beverages

Recipes featured on previous page:
Crab Crescent Loaf *page 4*
Stuffed Mushrooms *page 12*
Sweet Tea *page 17*

Appetizer Cups .... *Lill Stoltzfus*

1 (8 count) pkg. flaky biscuits
8 pieces bacon,
　fried and crumbled
1 medium tomato, chopped
1 small onion, chopped
3 oz. Swiss cheese, shredded
⅓ c. mayonnaise
½ tsp. dried basil

Cut biscuits in half, and put in tart pans to form crust. Mix remaining ingredients. Fill shells. Bake at 350° for 15 minutes.
　Yield: 16 appetizer cups.

Cauliflower Poppers .... *Gina Mast*

1 small head cauliflower
½ tsp. chili powder
½ tsp. ground cumin
½ tsp. salt
½ tsp. black pepper

Preheat oven to 400°. Coat a baking sheet with cooking spray. Cut cauliflower florets into bite-sized pieces (there should be about 4 cups.) Place cauliflower in a medium bowl and add cumin, chili powder, salt and pepper; toss well to coat. Spread cauliflower on prepared baking sheet and bake until tender, but not mushy, stirring halfway through. Bake around 10 minutes.
　Yield: 8 (½ cup) servings.

Cheese Ball .... *Ruth Weaver*

16 oz. cream cheese
1 c. shredded cheddar cheese
¾ Tbsp. Worcestershire sauce
¾ Tbsp. lemon juice
½ tsp. liquid smoke
1 tsp. minced onion
garlic salt
½ c. chopped nuts

Mix all ingredients except nuts. Form into a ball and roll in nuts or sprinkle nuts only on top. Serve with your favorite snack crackers.

Christmas Party Pinwheels .... *Elsie Yoder*

16 oz. cream cheese, softened
1 pkg. ranch dressing mix
½ c. minced red bell peppers
½ c. minced celery
¼ c. sliced green onions
¼ c. sliced stuffed olives
3-4 (10") flour tortillas

In a mixing bowl, beat cream cheese and dressing mix until smooth. Add red peppers, celery, onions, and olives; mix well. Spread about ¾ cup on each tortilla. Roll up tightly; wrap in plastic wrap. Refrigerate for at least 2 hours. Slice into ½" pieces. Good served with salsa.
Yield: 15-20 servings.

Christmas Popcorn .... *Lill Stoltzfus*

8 qt. popped-popcorn salted lightly
1 c. butter
½ c. Karo
9 oz. red hot cinnamon candies

Boil and stir butter, Karo and red hot cinnamon candies till red hots melt. Keep stirring as it burns easily. Stir into popcorn. Spread on greased cookie sheets. Bake at 250° for 1 hour stirring every 15 minutes. Store in a tin.
Note: This recipe was given to me by Rosie Mast.

Crab Crescent Loaf .... *LaVerda Weaver*

1 (8 oz.) tube crescent roll
6 oz. cream cheese, softened
⅓ c. chopped onions
½ tsp. dill weed
1 c. chopped imitation crab meat
1 egg yolk, beaten

On greased baking sheet, unroll crescent dough into one long rectangle. Seal seams and perforations. In a small mixing bowl, beat the cream cheese, onion and dill until blended. Spread mixture lengthwise over half of the dough to within ½" of edges. Top with crab meat. Fold dough over filling. Pinch seam to seal. Brush the top with egg yolk. Bake at 375° for 18-22 minutes or till golden brown.
Yield: 12 slices.

Fresh Fruit Dip .... *Rachel Kanagy*

8 oz. cream cheese
½ c. brown sugar
1 c. whipped topping
2 tsp. vanilla

Mix cream cheese and sugar together until smooth. Add vanilla and mix well. Mix in whipped topping. Serve with any type of fresh fruit.
Yield: 2 cups.

Fruit Sauce or Dip .... *Fannie Mae Kanagy*

¾ c. sugar
¼ c. flour
2 eggs, beaten
1 c. pineapple juice
¼ c. butter
3 c. Cool Whip

Mix sugar and flour until well blended in double boiler. Add eggs and juice. Cook in double boiler until very thick, stirring constantly. Add butter. Remove from heat and chill. Fold in Cool Whip. Serve with fresh fruit.

Note: Also good with drained fruit; fruit cocktail, pineapple chunks, or mandarin oranges.

Fresh Salsa .... *Lill Stoltzfus*

2 c. chopped tomatoes
2 c. chopped onions
1½ tsp. chopped
    fresh jalapeno pepper
1 lime, juiced
½ tsp. cumin
1 tsp. cilantro
1 avocado, diced
2 Tbsp. vinegar

Mix and enjoy with chips, or on meat.

Appetizers, Dips, Beverages

Tomato and Bell Pepper Salsa — *Susanna Kanagy*

3 med. tomatoes, chopped
1 med. bell pepper, chopped
6 green onions, chopped
1 jalapeno pepper,
   seeded and chopped
2 Tbsp. chopped cilantro
3 garlic cloves, minced
2 Tbsp. fresh lime juice
½ tsp. salt

Combine all ingredients. Serve with tortilla chips.
Yield: 12 servings.

Guacamole .... *Susanna Kanagy*

2 avocados, seeded,
   peeled and mashed
2 green onions, chopped
1 Tbsp. mayonnaise
1 Tbsp. lime juice
½ tsp. cumin
½ tsp. chili powder
¼ tsp. garlic salt

Combine all ingredients. Serve with tortilla chips.
Yield: 6-8 servings.

Hearty Calico Bean Dip .... *Gina Mast*

¾ lb. ground beef
1 (16 oz.) can baked beans
1 (15 oz.) can Great Northern
   Beans, rinsed and drained
1 (15 oz.) can kidney beans
½ lb. sliced bacon,
   crisp-cooked and crumbled
1 onion, chopped
½ c. packed brown sugar
½ c. ketchup
1 Tbsp. cider vinegar
1 tsp. yellow mustard
tortilla chips

Brown beef in large skillet over medium-high heat 6-8 minutes, stirring to break up meat. Drain fat. Transfer beef to slow cooker. Add all the beans, bacon onion, brown sugar, ketchup, vinegar, and mustard; mix well. Cover; cook on low for 4 hours or on high for 2 hours. Serve with tortilla chips.
Yield: 12 servings.

French Onion Hamburger Dip....*Susan Miller*

8 oz. cream cheese
12-16 oz. french onion dip
1 lb. hamburger, fried
1 (16 oz.) can taco sauce
1 green pepper, chopped
sliced mushrooms
black olives, sliced
salsa
grated cheese

Mix cream cheese and dip together and spread on bottom of 9"x13" pan. Mix hamburger and taco sauce, then spread over first layer. Layer next 5 ingredients in pan in order. Amounts of these last 5 ingredients may be varied or omitted as desired. Bake at 200° for 1 hour. Serve with corn chips.
Yield: 15 servings.

Hamburger Dip................*LaVerda Weaver*

2 lb. hamburger
1 lb. cheese, shredded
½ onion, chopped
¼ green pepper, chopped
⅛ tsp. red pepper
⅛ tsp. chili powder
⅛ tsp. garlic salt
2 pkg. taco seasoning
1 can cream of mushroom soup
2 cans tomato soup

Brown hamburger and add the rest of ingredients. Heat through. Serve with tortilla chips.

Mexican Corn Dip...............*Tammy Yoder*

1 (14.5 oz.) can whole kernel corn, drained
½ c. diced red bell peppers
½ c. diced green peppers
1 c. mayonnaise
1 c. shredded cheddar cheese
1 tsp. chili powder
½ tsp. ground black pepper
½ tsp. fresh parsley, chopped

Combine ingredients and mix well. Serve chilled with chili corn chips or ranch flavored chips.

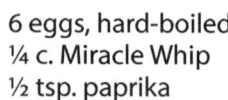

Party Deviled Eggs............ *Maryglenn Brown*

6 eggs, hard-boiled
¼ c. Miracle Whip
½ tsp. paprika

Peel and halve eggs. Scoop yolks out into bowl. Place whites onto serving platter. Mash yolks with fork. Add Miracle Whip and paprika. Stuff whites with yolk mixture. Garnish with paprika.

Pepperoni Rolls.................... *Rachel Kanagy*

½ of "Soft Potato Roll" recipe
2 eggs yolks
1 Tbsp. Parmesan cheese
1 tsp. parsley
1 tsp. oregano
½ tsp. garlic powder
¼ tsp. pepper
2 Tbsp. vegetable oil
pepperoni slices, quartered
mozzarella cheese

Mix roll dough as directed (see page 25). Roll to approximately ⅜" thickness (about 14"x20"). Stir next 7 ingredients together and spread over dough. Sprinkle pepperoni chips across the egg mixture. Roll up, then slice into 1" slices. Lay on baking sheet about ¼"–½" apart. Let rise for 1 hour. Bake 10–12 minutes at 350°. Garnish with mozzarella cheese and bake a few more minutes.
Yield: 20 rolls.

Pico De Gallo .... *Susanna Kanagy*

3 lg. tomatoes, chopped
½ c. chopped sweet onions
1–2 jalepenos, seeded and chopped
¼ c. chopped cilantro
3 Tbsp. fresh lime juice
1 tsp. salt
½ tsp. pepper

Combine all ingredients. Serve with tortilla chips.
Yield: 8–10 servings.

Pizza Dip .... Glenda Weaver

8 oz. cream cheese
½ c. sour cream
⅛ tsp. oregano
⅛ tsp. garlic powder
⅛ tsp. red pepper
½ c. pizza sauce
¾ c. peppers, (optional)
¼ c. onions, (optional)
pepperoni
shredded cheese

Mix first 5 ingredients and spread in a pie pan. Top with next 3 ingredients and bake at 350° for 10 minutes. Top with pepperoni and cheese. Bake 8–10 minutes longer. Serve warm with chips.

Pretzel Dip .... Susanna Kanagy

1 c. sour cream
1 c. mayonnaise
1 c. mustard
1 (1 oz.) pkg. ranch dressing mix
½ c. sugar

Combine all ingredients. Serve with pretzels.
Yield: 3 cups.

Sausage, Bean, and Spinach Dip Sheryl Kanagy

1 sweet onion, diced
1 red bell pepper, sliced
1 lb. ground pork sausage
2 garlic cloves, minced
1 tsp. fresh thyme, chopped
8 oz. cream cheese, softened
6 oz. fresh baby spinach, coarsely chopped
¼ tsp. salt
1 (15 oz.) can pinto beans, drained and rinsed
½ c. shredded Parmesan cheese

Preheat oven to 375°. Cook diced onions, bell peppers, and sausage in a large skillet. Drain. Stir in garlic and thyme. Cook 1 minute. Add cream cheese and cook, stirring constantly, until cream cheese is melted. Stir in spinach and salt. Cook, stirring constantly, until spinach is wilted. Gently stir in beans. Pour mixture into a 2 quart baking dish, sprinkle with Parmesan cheese. Bake at 375° for 18–20 minutes or until golden brown. Serve with tortilla chips.
Yield: about 6 cups.

Seasoned Pretzels .... *Renae Weaver*

1 c. vegetable oil
½ c. sour cream and onion powder
¼ c. sugar
1 tsp. lemon pepper
½ tsp. garlic powder
2 lb. Rold Gold pretzel twists

Mix all ingredients except pretzels. Pour over pretzels and toss to coat. Let set for several hours, stirring occasionally. Yield: 20 servings.

Seasoned Pretzels .... *Tammy Yoder*

2 lb. pretzels
½ c. vegetable oil
1 tsp. dill weed
1 tsp. garlic powder
1 tsp. lemon pepper
1 pkg. Hidden Valley ranch mix

Mix together. Bake at 350° for 30 minutes, stirring every 10 minutes.

Smoky Bacon Wraps .... *Alta Miller*

1 lb. bacon
1 lb. little smokies
1 c. brown sugar

Cut bacon slices in half. Wrap one piece around each smokie. Place on baking sheet, then sprinkle with brown sugar. Bake at 400° for 30–40 minutes or till bacon is crisp.

Note: Lining the baking sheet with foil before baking makes cleanup easier. Toothpicks may be inserted before baking, to hold bacon in place.

Sweet Little Smokies . . . . *Renae Weaver*

1 tube crescent roll
24 smokies
½ c. butter
½ c. chopped pecans
3 Tbsp. honey
3 Tbsp. brown sugar

Divide crescent roll into 24 pieces and wrap sausages. Place in a greased 9"x13" pan. Combine remaining ingredients in sauce pan and heat to dissolve sugar. Pour over sausages. Bake at 375° for 20 minutes.
Yield: 6-8 servings.

Southwestern Chicken Salad Spirals . . . .
Elsie Yoder

1 (7 oz.) jar roasted red bell peppers
2 c. cooked chicken, chopped
8 oz. cream cheese
1 env. Ranch buttermilk dressing mix
¼ c. ripe olives, chopped
½ c. diced onions
1 (4.5 oz.) can green chilies, chopped and drained
½ tsp. pepper
2 tsp. chopped cilantro
6 (8") flour tortillas

Drain roasted peppers well, by pressing between paper towels, then chop them. Add all the ingredients except the tortillas. Cover and chill 2 hours. Spoon evenly over tortillas, and roll up. Cut each roll into 5 slices, securing with wooden picks if necessary. Chill 2 hours, then serve. Good served with salsa.

Spinach Dip . . . . *Susan Miller*

1 c. mayonnaise
2 c. sour cream
4 oz. cream cheese
1 c. chopped celery
½ c. chopped onions
1 Tbsp. parsley flakes
½ tsp. pepper
1 pkg. Knorr Vegetable soup mix
1 (10 oz.) pkg. frozen spinach, chopped

Combine mayonnaise, sour cream and cream cheese. Add celery, onions, parsley flakes, pepper and soup mix. Thaw spinach and drain very well, then add to mayonnaise mixture. Serve with crackers or in a round bread bowl with chunks of bread.

Stuffed Mushrooms........... Lori Miller

18 small mushrooms
4 oz. smoked salmon
¾ oz. cream cheese
¾ c. sour cream
2 Tbsp. bread crumbs
¾ tsp. lemon juice
dash of parsley
grated Parmesan cheese

Mix everything together and stuff mushrooms before baking. Drizzle three tablespoons butter and ½ teaspoon garlic powder over mushrooms. Bake at 350° for 25 minutes.

Note: Very good! Can also add some onion and Swiss cheese to mixture if desired.

Taco Dip........... Fern Weaver

32 oz. cream cheese
32 oz. sour cream
1 pkg. taco seasoning mix
1 tsp. onion powder
green peppers
tomatoes
shredded cheese

Mix first four ingredients. Spread on serving plate. Top with green peppers, tomatoes and cheese. Serve with chips.

Tomato Bacon Cups........... Sheryl Kanagy

1 (10 oz.) can flaky biscuits
¼ c. mayonnaise
1 medium tomato, diced
1 small onion, diced
8 slices bacon,
   fried and crumbled
3 oz. shredded Swiss cheese
⅛ tsp. dry basil

Separate biscuits in layers, enough to fill a two dozen mini muffin pan. Press biscuit dough down and up sides of each mini muffin cup. Mix together remaining ingredients and put a small amount in each muffin cup. Bake at 375° for 12–15 minutes.
Yield: 24 cups.

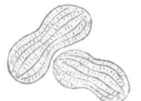

Vegetable Dip .... *Alta Miller*

8 oz. cream cheese
1 c. mayonnaise
½ c. sour cream
2 beef bouillon cubes
2 Tbsp. chopped onions

Beat cream cheese. Dissolve bouillon cubes in 1 tablespoon boiling water. Add all remaining ingredients to cream cheese and beat well.

Vegetable Dip .... *Fern Weaver*

2 beef bouillon cubes
¼ c. water
1 c. mayonnaise
2 Tbsp. minced onions
8 oz. cream cheese

Dissolve beef bouillon in water. Mix all together and refrigerate. Yield: 2½ cups.

Appetizers, Dips, Beverages

Cappuccino .... *Glenda Weaver*

2 c. coffee creamer
2 c. french vanilla coffee creamer
2 c. dry milk
3 Tbsp. Nesquik
¾ c. instant coffee
1½ c. sugar
1½ c. powdered sugar
½ tsp. salt
½ tsp. cinnamon
⅛ tsp. nutmeg

Mix all of the ingredients together. To serve, add 3 tablespoons of dry mix to a mug of hot water.

Note: I like to use about half of the sugar.

Coffee Party Punch .... *Rachel Kanagy*

¾ c. instant coffee
½ c. sugar
1 c. hot water
2 qt. milk
1 qt. chocolate ice cream
1 qt. vanilla ice cream

Mix coffee and sugar in water until dissolved. Let cool. About ½ hour before serving time, add milk and scoops of ice cream. Ice cream will become soft and creamy and can be served from a punch bowl.
Yield: about 1 gallon.

Créme de Menthe .... *Sheryl Kanagy*

½ c. water
6 small York mint patties
¼ c. sugar
2 c. strong brewed coffee
2 c. half and half
whipped cream to garnish

Mix all ingredients together and bring to a boil. Stir constantly until York patties are melted. Serve with whipped cream.
Yield: 4 servings

Hot Chocolate .... *Glenda Weaver*

2 Tbsp. cocoa
1 c. sugar
1 c. water
2 tsp. vanilla
2½ qt. milk

Heat first four ingredients, stirring occasionally until boiling. Add milk. Heat thoroughly.
Yield: 8 servings

Iced Coffee .... *Glenda Weaver and Katelyn Weaver*

1½ c. water
¾ c. sugar
1–1½ Tbsp. instant coffee
ice
milk
1–1½ Tbsp. vanilla
whipped topping (optional)
caramel syrup (optional)

Bring water to a boil. Dissolve sugar and coffee in water and pour into half gallon jug. Add ice until half full and fill to top with milk. Add vanilla and stir.
Note: May serve with whipped topping and caramel syrup.
Yield: 2 quarts or 8–10 servings.

Iced Coffee........... *Renae Weaver and Gina Mast*

1¾ c. sugar
5 Tbsp. instant coffee granules
3 c. boiling water
ice cubes
milk
3–4 Tbsp. vanilla

Dissolve sugar and coffee in boiling water. Pour into gallon pitcher. Fill with ice cubes until pitcher is half full. Add milk to fill pitcher. Add vanilla and stir.
Yield: 1 gallon or 10 servings

Frozen Coffee Drink............... *Tammy Yoder*

Syrup Concentrate:

2 c. boiling water
1 c. sugar
½ c. instant coffee
1 tsp. vanilla

Serving Ingredients:

½ c. syrup concentrate
2 scoops vanilla ice cream
½ c. milk
½ c. brewed coffee, room temperature
dash of caramel syrup

In a saucepan, stir together syrup ingredients. Let cool a little.
Serving Ingredients: In a blender, put syrup concentrate, ice cream, milk, coffee and caramel. Fill with ice and blend well. Garnish with whipped topping.
Note: Store syrup concentrate in refrigerator for up to 1 week.
Yield: 4 (8 oz.) servings

Mocha Shake..................... *Glenda Weaver*

¼ c. water
2 Tbsp. chocolate syrup
2 tsp. instant coffee
¾ c. milk
2½ c. vanilla ice cream

In blender, combine water, chocolate syrup, coffee, and milk. Cover and blend on low speed. Add ice cream and blend until smooth.
Yield: 2 servings.

Chai Tea Latte .... *Tammy Yoder*

2 c. water
1 Lipton tea bag
1 cinnamon stick
⅛ tsp. nutmeg
2½ c. milk
1 tsp. vanilla
⅓ c. sugar
Cool Whip
cinnamon

Combine water, tea, cinnamon stick and nutmeg. Bring to a boil. Reduce heat, cover and simmer for five minutes. Whisk in milk and boil one minute. Add sugar and vanilla, stir until dissolved. Garnish with whipped cream and cinnamon.

Pumpkin Spice Latte .... *Valetta Yoder*

Syrup Concentrate:

1½ c. water
1½ c. sugar
4 cinnamon sticks or
  1 Tbsp. cinnamon
½ tsp. cloves
½ tsp. ginger
1 tsp. nutmeg
3 Tbsp. canned pumpkin

Serving Ingredients:
For 1 serving:

1 c. hot milk
2–4 Tbsp. strong
  brewed coffee
2 Tbsp. syrup concentrate
whipped cream

For 8 Servings:

8 c. hot milk
2 c. strong brewed coffee
1 c. syrup concentrate
whipped cream

Dissolve water and sugar. Add remaining ingredients. Cook and stir 5–8 minutes, but do not boil mixture.

Note: This can be stored in refrigerator for a long period of time.

Serving Ingredients: Combine milk, coffee, and syrup concentrate. Serve with whipped cream.

Paul Harvey Punch .... *Lori Miller*

2 c. boiling water
¾ c. honey
4 c. cranberry juice cocktail
2 c. orange juice
1 c. lemon juice
1 qt. ginger ale

Mix water and honey. Chill, then add rest of ingredients. Before serving, add ginger ale.

Pineapple Tea Drink .... *Susan Miller*

6 small (or 2 family size) Lipton tea or Tetley tea bags
2 c. boiling water
1 c. sugar
6 Tbsp. lemon juice
1 tsp. vanilla
46 oz. pineapple juice
2–liter 7-Up or Sprite

Brew tea bags in boiling water. Add sugar and stir. Add lemon juice and vanilla. Chill thoroughly. Add pineapple juice. Just before serving add 7-Up or Sprite. Serve with lots of ice.

Yield: approximately 10 servings

Sweet Tea .... *Susanna Kanagy*

4 family size tea bags (Lipton, Luzianne, or Tetley)
1½ c. sugar
ice
lemon wedges (optional)

Pour two quarts boiling water over tea bags in a heat proof pitcher. Let steep 5–10 minutes. Remove tea bags. Fill a one gallon pitcher half full with ice. Add sugar. Pour tea over sugar and ice. Add enough water to make one gallon. Stir well. To serve fill glasses with ice. Pour tea over ice in glasses and garnish with lemon wedges if desired.

Yield: 10–12 servings.

Appetizers, Dips, Beverages

Strawberry Blender.............. *Rachel Kanagy*

¼ c. lemon juice
1 c. chopped strawberries, fresh or frozen,
¼–½ c. sugar
1½ c. water
15–18 ice cubes
12 oz. Sprite

Blend first five ingredients together until smooth. Add Sprite. Serve immediately. Fills a 6 cup blender.

Strawberry Daquiri............... *Glenda Weaver*

2 c. strawberries
3 c. crushed ice
¼ c. sugar (no sugar if strawberries are sweetened)
½ c. lemon juice
¾ c. Sprite

Mix well in blender, then add Sprite.
Note: Works well to make a few hours ahead and freeze, stirring occasionally.
Yield: about 6 cups.

Strawberry Pineapple Smoothie. *Tammy Yoder*

1 c. frozen strawberries
¾ c. milk
¾ c. fresh pineapple chunks
½ c. vanilla yogurt
2 Tbsp. sugar
½ tsp. vanilla
ice cubes

Mix ingredients in blender. Add ice cubes until right consistency. Garnish with whipped topping and a fresh pineapple wedge.
Note: Makes a delicious summertime drink.
Yield: 2-4 servings.

Wedding Punch .... *LaVerda Weaver*

46 oz. pineapple juice
24 oz. frozen lemonade conc.
12 oz. frozen limeade conc.
2 (2 liter) 7-Up
1½ c. water
1 c. sugar
red food coloring
1 bag ice
1 quart pineapple sherbet

Mix all ingredients together, except sherbet. Adding food coloring till it is a nice pink color. Add sherbet just before serving.

Note: It is also good without the sherbet.

Yield: 3 gallons.

Don't feel discouraged; even the sun has a sinking spell every night, but rises again in the morning.

A Taste of Blackville

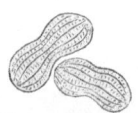

Breakfast, Breads

Recipe featured on previous page:
Challah Bread *page 24*

Wilbur Martha's Bread............. *Fern Weaver*

4½ c. milk
¾ c. vegetable oil
1½ c. warm water
6 Tbsp. yeast
9 Tbsp. sugar or honey
3 Tbsp. salt
2 c. whole wheat flour
5 lb. bread flour

Heat milk to boiling point, then add oil and let cool to lukewarm. Dissolve yeast in water; add whole wheat flour. Add remaining ingredients. Knead until dough becomes nice and smooth, and no longer sticky. Let rise until double in size, then shape and put in pans—1¼ pounds in each bread pan. Let rise until double in size. Bake at 300° for 30 minutes or until nice and brown. Butter tops of loaves.
Yield: 7-8 loaves

Butter Horns...................... *Glenda Weaver*

4 c. flour
½ c. sugar
1 tsp. salt
1 c. cold butter or shortening
1 Tbsp. yeast
¼ c. cold water
¾ c. warm milk
1 egg, beaten
4 Tbsp. melted butter, divided

Combine flour, sugar and salt in a large bowl. Cut in butter until mixture resembles coarse crumbs. In another bowl, dissolve yeast in water. Add to mixture. Add milk and egg; mix well. Cover and refrigerate overnight. Divide dough into four portions. Roll one portion into a 12" circle on a floured surface. Brush with 1 tablespoon melted butter. Cut into 12 pie shaped wedges. Beginning with the wide end, roll up and place on greased baking sheets. Repeat with remaining dough. Cover and let rise in a warm place until nearly doubled (about 1 hour). Bake at 375° for 10–12 minutes or until golden brown.
Yield: 48 rolls.

Butter Horns ...... *Susanna Kanagy and Renae Weaver*

1 Tbsp. yeast
1 c. warm water
½ c. sugar
3 eggs, beaten
½ c. melted butter or vegetable oil
1 tsp. salt
5 c. bread flour

Dissolve yeast in warm water. Add sugar, eggs, butter, salt and 2 cups flour. Knead in remaining flour. Cover and refrigerate overnight. Divide dough in half. Roll each half into a 12" circle. Cut each into 16 wedges. Roll up starting at wide end. Place on greased baking sheet and let rise 2–3 hours. Bake at 350°–375° for 15 minutes. Butter tops and serve warm.

Note: Renae divides her dough in four parts and cuts each into eight wedges.
Yield: 32 rolls.

Challah Bread .... *Alta Miller and Lori Miller*

2 Tbsp. yeast
2 c. warm water
¼ c. sugar
¼ c. shortening or butter
3 eggs
2 tsp. salt
6½–7½ c. flour, divided
1 beaten egg (to brush top)
sesame seeds

Mix yeast, water, sugar and shortening. Add eggs one at a time. Add 3 cups flour and salt, then beat for 2 minutes. Let rise for 30 minutes or till spongy. Add remaining flour and knead. Let rise. Divide into 6 pieces. Roll each piece into a rope. Braid three ropes together. Place on greased cookie sheet, then let rise. Before baking, brush with beaten egg and sprinkle with sesame seeds. Bake at 375° for 40–45 minutes, or until golden brown. Bread will be crusty.

Note: this is a traditional Jewish Sabbath bread.
Yield: 20 servings.

Dinner Rolls................... *Fannie Mae Kanagy*

2 Tbsp. yeast
1 c. warm water
½ c. sugar
½ c. butter
2 eggs, beaten
1½ tsp. salt
1 c. scalded milk, cooled
6–7 c. flour
1 c. whole wheat flour

Dissolve yeast in water. Beat sugar and butter with mixer. Add eggs and salt. Add cooled milk and part of flour and beat. Add yeast mixture and remaining flour and stir. Work lightly. Let rise till double, about 2 hours. Roll out to ¾" thick and cut with biscuit cutter or pinch off small amount of dough with greased hands to make small rolls. Let rise again. Bake at 340° for 15 minutes.
Yield: 58 small rolls.

Soft Potato Rolls................. *Rachel Kanagy*

½ c. warm water
2 Tbsp. yeast
2 c. warm milk
½ c. margarine, softened
½ c. sugar
2 tsp. salt
½ c. instant potato flakes
2 eggs
6½–7 c. white bread flour

Dissolve yeast in warm water. Let set until bubbly. Add next six ingredients. Add 2 cups flour and mix well. Add remaining flour until dough is slightly sticky, but able to be kneaded. Continue kneading dough for 10 minutes. Let rise in greased bowl until double in bulk. Shape into balls and place on greased baking sheet. Let rise until rolls are at least double in size. Bake at 350° for 12–15 minutes, or until tops are brown. Brush tops with butter immediately after removing from oven.
Note: I use this basic roll recipe for cinnamon rolls, stromboli, and pepperoni rolls (see page 8).
Yield: approximately 40 rolls.

French Bread .... *Rachel Kanagy*

1¼ c. warm water
1 Tbsp. yeast
1 Tbsp. sugar
1 Tbsp. vegetable oil
1 tsp. salt
3-4 c. white bread flour

Dissolve yeast and sugar in warm water. Add oil, salt and 3 cups flour. Add remaining flour slowly until dough forms a ball and is only slightly sticky. Knead well. Form into loaf and place on greased baking sheet. Cut several slash marks at an angle across top of loaf with a sharp knife. Let rise until double in size. Bake at 350° for 15–20 minutes. Brush top with butter after removing from oven.
Yield: 8-10 servings.

Skillet Cornbread .... *Susanna Kanagy*

3 Tbsp. butter
½ c. butter, softened
½ c. sugar
2 eggs, beaten
1 c. milk
1¾ c. flour
3 tsp. baking powder
¼ tsp. salt
1 c. cornmeal
butter
honey

Preheat over to 350°. In a 10" cast iron skillet, place 3 tablespoons butter. Set in oven to melt while preparing batter. In a bowl, beat ½ cup butter and sugar until creamy. Add eggs and milk, mix well. Combine flour, baking powder and salt. Add to creamed mixture. Stir in cornmeal. Pour batter into heated skillet and bake 20–30 minutes or until toothpick inserted in center comes out clean. Serve with butter and honey.
Yield: 6–8 servings.

Italian Bread Bowls .... *Alta Miller*

2½ c. warm water
2 Tbsp. yeast
2 tsp. salt
2 Tbsp. vegetable oil
7 c. flour
1 Tbsp. cornmeal
1 egg white
1 Tbsp. water

Mix 2½ cup water and yeast in large bowl. Let set 5 minutes, then stir in salt and oil. Add flour gradually, beating till soft dough forms. Turn onto a floured surface. Knead till smooth and elastic (4–6 minutes). Place in greased bowl and let rise till double. Punch down and divide into eight portions. Shape each into a 4" round loaf. Place on greased baking sheets sprinkled with cornmeal. Let rise till double. Mix egg white and 1 tablespoon water, and brush over loaves. Bake at 400° for 15 minutes. Brush again with egg mixture, then bake 10–15 minutes more. Cool. To use: cut ½" thick slice from top of each loaf. Scoop out centers, leaving ¾" thick shells.

Note: Loaves can be frozen up to one month. They are great with clam chowder.

Yield: 8 servings.

Basic Crepes .... *Tammy Yoder*

1½ c. milk
4 eggs
1 c. all-purpose flour
1½ tsp. sugar
⅛ tsp. salt
8 tsp. butter

Whisk together milk and eggs. Add flour, sugar and salt. Mix well. Refrigerate one hour. In small non-stick skillet, melt 1 teaspoon butter. Pour 2 tablespoons dough into pan. Cook about 20 seconds until it looks "dry". Repeat until all crepes are made.

Note: Do not skip refrigerating dough or the crepes will not set up right.

Flour Tortillas .... *Glenda Weaver*

2½ c. flour
½ c. cornmeal
3 tsp. baking powder
1 tsp. salt
¼ c. vegetable oil
1 c. warm water

Combine dry ingredients and oil in bowl. Add water and mix well. Turn out on a floured surface and knead until soft and no longer sticky. Roll dough into balls about 1½" in diameter. On floured surface, roll out balls as thin as possible. Cook on a hot, ungreased griddle, until lightly browned on both sides. As tortillas are done, place in a cloth lined bowl and cover to keep warm and moist.
Yield: about 16 tortillas.

Chipa Guasú .... *Valetta Yoder*

1 onion, chopped
6 c. whole kernel corn
milk
1 c. vegetable oil or butter
3 eggs
3 c. Paraguayan cheese or
   Swiss cheese
1 c. plain yogurt or sour cream
1 Tbsp. salt

Sauté the onion with a little butter. Place corn in blender. Add enough milk to blend corn to smooth consistency. Mix all ingredients together. Pour in 9"x13" pan. Bake at 350° for approximately 1 hour.

Golden Garlic Bread .... *Alta Miller*

½ c. butter, softened
¼ c. mayonnaise
¼ c. grated Parmesan cheese
1½ c. shredded
   cheddar cheese
3 green onions,
   chopped (optional)
1 tsp. Italian seasoning
1 tsp. garlic powder
1–1 lb. loaf French bread

Mix first seven ingredients. Split bread in half, then spread mixture on both halves. Bake at 350° for approximately 20 minutes, or till top is golden and bubbly.
Yield: 12-15 servings.

Jalapeño Cheddar Bread ...... *Susanna Kanagy*

2 Tbsp. yeast
2 c. warm water
½ c. sugar
1 Tbsp. salt
2 eggs
¼ c. vegetable oil
2 Jalapeño peppers, chopped (reserving seeds of 1 pepper)
1 Tbsp. instant minced onion
½ c. shredded cheddar cheese
½ tsp. garlic powder
6½–7 c. bread flour

Dissolve yeast in warm water. Stir in sugar, salt, eggs, oil, peppers, reserved seeds, onion, cheese, garlic powder and 3 cups flour. Beat until smooth. Add remaining flour. Beat until smooth and elastic. Cover and let rise 1 hour or until double. Divide into four equal parts. Shape into French style loaves. Place on greased baking sheets and let rise until doubled. Bake at 350° for 20–25 minutes.
Yield: 4 loaves.

Pizza Hut Bread Sticks .... *Glenda Weaver*

1½ c. warm water
1 Tbsp. yeast
1 Tbsp. vegetable oil
1 Tbsp. sugar
1 tsp. salt
4 c. flour

Butter Mixture:

½ c. butter, melted
3 Tbsp. olive oil
3 Tbsp. Parmesan cheese
1 tsp. garlic powder
1 Tbsp. dried parsley
2–3 Tbsp. Italian seasoning

Dissolve yeast in warm water; add oil, sugar and salt. Stir in flour until it is too stiff to stir with a spoon. Put onto a floured surface and knead several times. Let rise until double. Roll out on a large cookie sheet. Mix all butter mixture ingredients together. Cut into bread sticks and spread butter mixture across top. Let rise for 20–30 minutes. Sprinkle with a bit of Parmesan cheese. Bake at 350° for about 15–18 minutes or until golden brown.
Yield: 15 servings.

Pizza Hut Bread Sticks .... *LaVerda Weaver*

Dough:

1½ c. warm water
1 Tbsp. sugar
3 Tbsp. vegetable oil
¾ c. melted butter
1 Tbsp. yeast
1¼ tsp. salt
4 c. flour

Seasonings:

1 Tbsp. garlic powder
3 Tbsp. Parmesan cheese
1 Tbsp. dried parsley
1 Tbsp. Italian seasoning

Mix dough. Let rise till double in size. Roll out in large squares. and cut into strips. Place on cookie sheet, brush with melted butter. Mix seasonings and sprinkle on bread sticks. Bake at 350° till done. Serve with warm pizza sauce or cheese sauce.

Red Lobster Biscuits .... *Renae Weaver*

2 c. Bisquick baking mix
½ c. shredded cheddar cheese
⅔ c. milk
½ c. melted butter, divided
½ tsp. garlic powder, divided

Mix Bisquick, cheese and milk into a soft dough. Add ¼ cup melted butter and ¼ teaspoon garlic powder. Mix well. Spoon onto a greased baking pan. Smooth down tops. Bake at 425° for 8–10 minutes. Combine remaining butter and garlic powder, brush on top of baked biscuits.

Yield: 10 biscuits.

Pizza Hut Pizza Crust .... *Gina Mast*

1 Tbsp. yeast
1⅓ c. warm water
1 Tbsp. sugar
1½ Tbsp. vegetable oil
¾ tsp. salt
⅛ tsp. garlic powder
¼ tsp. oregano
3½ c. flour

Mix like bread dough. You don't have to let it rise, but it is alright if you do. Grease one pizza pan. Sprinkle pan with garlic salt. Spread dough in pan and prick dough with a fork. Put on your favorite toppings. Bake at 450° for 10 minutes. The high heat makes it crisp.

Pizza Crust .... *Esther Stoltzfus*

¼ c. vegetable oil
1 egg
2 Tbsp. sugar
1 tsp. salt
1 c. water
1 Tbsp. yeast
3 c. flour

Mix all ingredients together except the flour. Add flour slowly to make a soft dough. More flour may be needed. Let rise. Roll out in a greased 13"x18" cookie sheet. Bake at 350° till light brown.

Soft Pretzels .... *Renae Weaver*

1¼ c. warm water
1 Tbsp. yeast
¼ c. brown sugar
3½ c. flour
4 tsp. baking soda
½ c. cold water
pretzel salt
melted butter

Dissolve yeast in water. Add sugar and flour, knead well. Let rise 20 minutes. Divide into twelve pieces and shape into pretzels. Combine soda and water. Dip pretzels in water and place on well greased cookie sheets. Sprinkle with pretzel salt. Bake at 500° for 5–7 minutes. Brush with melted butter. Yield: 4-6 servings.

Lemon Poppy Seed Bread .... *Valetta Yoder*

½ c. butter, softened
1 c. sugar
2 eggs
1½ c. flour
1 tsp. baking powder
⅔ c. milk
2 tsp. poppy seeds
1 tsp. vanilla
1 tsp. lemon flavoring

Glaze:

½ c. powdered sugar
½ tsp. lemon flavoring
water

Mix together butter, sugar, and eggs. Add flour and baking powder and mix well. Beat in milk. Stir in poppy seeds and flavorings until just combined. Bake at 350° in 2 greased and floured bread pans.

Glaze: Mix together, adding enough water to make glaze a pouring consistency. Pour over bread while still warm.

Pecan Lemon Loaf .... *Susan Miller*

½ c. butter, softened
1 c. sugar
2 eggs
2 c. all-purpose flour
1 tsp. baking powder
½ tsp. salt
¾ c. sour cream
1 c. chopped pecans, toasted
1 Tbsp. lemon zest

Glaze:

¼ c. lemon juice
½ c. sugar

Cream butter and sugar till light and fluffy. Add eggs and mix well. Combine flour, baking powder and salt. Add to creamed mixture alternately with sour cream. Fold in pecans and lemon zest. Bake in a greased 9"x3"x5" loaf pan for 50–60 minutes at 350° or until toothpick comes out clean.

Glaze: In small saucepan: combine lemon juice and sugar. Cook and stir till sugar is dissolved. Pour over warm bread. Cool before removing from pan.

Note: Optional—Drizzle with your favorite glaze and sprinkle with poppy seeds.

Yield: 8 servings.

Cinnamon Rolls..................... *Fern Weaver*

2 c. milk, scalded
¼ c. Crisco or butter
1 Tbsp. salt
¾ c. sugar
2 eggs
2½ Tbsp. yeast
1 c. warm water
8 c. bread flour (more or less)

Toppings:

softened butter
brown sugar
cinnamon

Heat milk, add Crisco or butter and let cool to lukewarm. Add salt, sugar and eggs. Put yeast in water. Let set a few minutes, then add to other mixture. Add bread flour until dough is soft, but slightly sticky yet. Let rise till double in size. Roll out and spread with butter. Sprinkle brown sugar and cinnamon on top. Roll up like a jelly roll, and cut in 1" slices. Put in pans, and let rise 20 minutes. Bake at 300° for 25 minutes. Frost with your favorite frosting.
Note: Our family prefers caramel frosting.

Doughnuts........................... *Lill Stoltzfus*

3–4 potatoes mashed
1 qt. milk, scalded
3 Tbsp. yeast
1 c. lukewarm water
1 c. shortening
2 c. sugar
2 c. water
3 Tbsp. salt
2 eggs, beaten
20 c. flour (approximately)

Glaze:

2 tsp. Karo
3 Tbsp. hot water
1½ c. powdered sugar
   (more or less)
1 tsp. vanilla

Cook potatoes till soft then mash. Cool potatoes and milk to lukewarm. Add water, shortening, sugar and salt. Stir in dissolved yeast. Add eggs. Stir in 2 cups flour and let stand 10 minutes, then continue to add flour 2 cups at a time and stir in. Knead dough (should be sticky). Cover and let rise till double. Knead down. Roll out ½" thick, cut with doughnut cutter or biscuit cutter. Let rise. Deep fat fry at 350° till golden brown. Dip in glaze. Dry on rods over cookie sheets.
Note: My mom often made these.
Yield: approximately 100 doughnuts.

Easy Donuts............ *Noah Schrock*

1 can Pillsbury buttermilk biscuits
Canola oil to deep fat fry

Poke a hole in the middle of each biscuit. Fry in hot oil till browned on each side. Make a glaze with powdered sugar, water and vanilla. Glaze donuts. Enjoy!
Yield: 10 donuts.

Orange Twists... *Fannie Mae Kanagy and Lill Stoltzfus*

1 c. lukewarm water
3 Tbsp. yeast
1 tsp. sugar
1 c. orange juice, warmed
½ c. butter, softened
⅔ c. sugar
2 eggs
1½ tsp. salt
6½ c. flour

Glaze:

1 lb. powdered sugar
rind and juice from 2 oranges
⅛ tsp. orange flavoring
yellow food coloring

Mix water, yeast and sugar in small bowl, and set aside. Beat butter, sugar, eggs and salt till light and fluffy. Add orange juice, yeast mixture, and part of flour and beat. Add remainder of flour and stir or knead till soft dough forms and is a little sticky. Let rise 1 hour. Roll out to ⅝" thickness. Cut with donut cutter and twist one time. Let rise until double and fry in hot oil. Mix glaze ingredients adding only enough orange juice to make a thick glaze. Dip twists. Cool on racks.
Yield: about 3 dozen.

Cheese Fruit Braid .... *Rachel Kanagy*

¼ c. sugar
2½ c. flour
¼ tsp. salt
½ c. butter
1½ tsp. yeast
½ c. water
1 large egg, beaten

Filling:

6 oz. cream cheese
¼ c. sugar
1 Tbsp. butter
1 tsp. lemon juice
1½ c. pie filling

Mix sugar, flour, and salt. Cut in butter. Mix yeast and water in a separate bowl until dissolved. Add egg and mix well. Mix liquid ingredients into dry ingredients and fold-knead until mixed. Do not over knead, just a little more than pie crust, but not as much as rolls! Refrigerate 5–6 hours or overnight. In a pinch, you can freeze 1–2 hours. Form 2 balls. Dough will be sticky, so sprinkle rolling surface liberally with flour. Roll each into a 9"x12" rectangle approximately ¼" thick. Mix first four filling ingredients together. Divide filling in half and spread down the center of each rectangle. Next, spread each with ¾ cup fruit filling of your choice. Slash strips along both the sides and bring to center, braiding alternately. May need some water to make dough stick to each other. Transfer to greased baking sheet. Let rise until slightly puffy, about 1 hour. Bake at 350° for 10–12 minutes. Glaze with powdered sugar glaze if desired.

Sticky Quickies .... Lori Miller

¾ c. milk
½ c. water
¼ c. vegetable oil
1 tsp. salt
¼ c. sugar
2 Tbsp. yeast
1 egg
3¼ c. flour

Topping:

¾ c. butter
1 c. brown sugar
1 tsp. cinnamon
1 Tbsp. Karo
1 Tbsp. water
¾ c. chopped nuts (optional)

Heat milk, water, oil, salt and sugar till lukewarm, then add yeast, egg and 1½ cup flour. Stir. Then add rest of flour. Let rise for 30 minutes. Melt butter. Add next 4 ingredients and mix until smooth. Add nuts if desired. Pour into a 9"x13" pan. Stir batter and drop by tablespoons on top of topping. Bake at 375° for 15–20 minutes. Cool 1 minute, then invert onto a serving platter.
Yield: 24 servings.

Swedish Tea Ring .... Lori Miller

1 Tbsp. yeast
1 c. warm water
¼ c. sugar
1 tsp. salt
3 Tbsp. butter
1 egg
3¼–3½ c. flour

Frosting:

¼ c. butter
¼ c. sugar
2 Tbsp. milk
1 tsp. vanilla
powdered sugar

Dissolve yeast, sugar and salt in warm water; add rest of ingredients. Let rise until double. Roll in a rectangle. Spread with butter, brown sugar and cinnamon. Roll up and place on a greased cookie sheet with seam side down. Pinch ends together. Make cuts halfway into center of ring 1" apart and lay on side. Let rise till double. Bake at 350° for 20 minutes. Let cool and then frost.
Frosting: Cook 5 minutes. Cool and add powdered sugar till right consistency to spread.

Blueberry Coffee Cake .... *Glenda Weaver*

1 egg
⅔ c. sugar
½ c. vegetable oil
½ tsp. vanilla
1½ c. flour
2 tsp. baking powder
½ tsp. salt
½ c. milk
1½ c. blueberries

Topping:

½ c. brown sugar
½ tsp. cinnamon
⅓ c. flour
¼ c. butter, melted
½ c. chopped nuts (optional)

Glaze:

1 c. powdered sugar
2 Tbsp. milk

Combine first four ingredients. Beat until fluffy. Mix together flour, baking powder, and salt. Add alternately with milk. Fold in blueberries and pour into a greased 9"x9" pan. Put topping on and bake at 350° for 30 minutes.

Note: This recipe makes a 9"x9" pan very full. For better results, take out enough batter to make a muffin along with the coffee cake.

Coffee Cake .... *Fern Weaver*

1 box yellow cake mix
1 (3 oz.) box instant vanilla pudding
4 eggs
¾ c. vegetable oil
¾ c. water
1 tsp. cinnamon
¾ c. brown sugar

Glaze:

1 c. powdered sugar
1 Tbsp. milk

Mix first five ingredients. Put half of batter in a greased bundt pan. Mix cinnamon and sugar. Spread half of sugar mixture on batter. Put the rest of batter in pan and sprinkle with the rest of sugar mixture. Bake at 325° for 45 minutes. Mix glaze ingredients and pour over coffee cake.

Coffee Cake .... *LaVerda Weaver*

1 Duncan Hines yellow cake mix
2 (3 oz.) boxes instant vanilla pudding
5 eggs
1 c. water
¾ c. vegetable oil
2 tsp. vanilla
½ c. sugar
3–4 tsp. cinnamon

Mix first 6 ingredients. Pour ⅓ of batter into a greased tube pan or bundt pan. Mix sugar and cinnamon together, Sprinkle with ½ of the sugar mixture. Pour ⅓ more of batter, and sprinkle remaining sugar mixture. Pour last of batter on. Using a knife, cut through batter several times. Bake at 325° for 1 hour or until done.

Easy Cinnamon Coffee Cake .. *Rachel Kanagy*

6 Tbsp. vegetable oil
1½ c. milk
1½ c. sugar
3 tsp. baking powder
1 tsp. salt
3 c. flour

Topping:
¾ c. brown sugar
2 tsp. cinnamon
6 Tbsp. butter, chunked

Glaze:
1 c. powdered sugar
½ tsp. vanilla
pinch of salt
1–2 Tbsp. milk

Combine oil and milk. In a separate bowl, mix dry ingredients together. Whisk liquids into dry ingredients until moistened. Pour into a greased 9"x13" pan. Combine cinnamon and sugar and sprinkle over top of batter. Dot the butter over the sugar mixture. Bake at 350° for 20–25 minutes. Let cool 15 minutes and drizzle with glaze.

Note: I like to make this when I have overnight company. I put all the dry ingredients in a bowl the night before. In the morning, I mix in the oil and milk and pop it in the oven along with a casserole.
Yield: 20 servings.

German Coffee Cake .... *Alta Miller*

1 c. butter
1½ c. sugar
1 tsp. vanilla
½ tsp. salt
3 eggs
2 c. flour
1 can cherry or blueberry pie filling

Cream butter, sugar, vanilla, salt and eggs. Beat well. Stir in flour. Spread all but 1 cup batter in bottom of 9"x13" pan. Top with pie filling. Drop remaining batter on top of filling. Bake for 45 minutes at 350° or until golden. While still warm, drizzle with your favorite glaze.
Yield: 20 servings.

Love never seeks to get away with doing the bare minimum.

Cream Cheese Danish............Lill Stoltzfus

½ c. warm water
2 Tbsp. yeast
1 tsp. sugar
1 c. sour cream
½ c. butter
½ c. sugar
1 tsp. salt
2 eggs, beaten
4 c. flour

Cream Cheese Filling:

16 oz. cream cheese
¼ c. sugar
1 egg, beaten
½ tsp. salt
2 tsp. vanilla

Icing:

4½ Tbsp. butter
6 Tbsp. milk
¾ c. sugar
1½ c. powdered sugar
   (approximately)
dash of salt
½ tsp. vanilla

Combine and stir water, yeast and 1 teaspoon sugar until dissolved. Set aside. Heat sour cream on low until almost bubbly. Add butter, ½ cup sugar and salt to sour cream, stirring until dissolved. Cool to lukewarm. Add eggs to the sour cream mixture, then combine with yeast mixture. Add flour and mix well. Cover and refrigerate overnight. Divide dough into four equal portions. Roll out each portion on a floured surface into a 12"x18" rectangle. Spread ¼ of cream cheese filling in center of each rectangle. Cut 2" slits into dough, 1" apart on each side. Fold toward middle and criss cross to form top. Cover and let rise until double. Bake at 350° for 12–15 minutes. Spread icing on loaves.

Cream Cheese Filling: Beat cream cheese. Add sugar and beat. Add rest of ingredients, stirring until creamy.

Icing: Mix first three ingredients. Boil for 2–3 minutes. Cool; add rest of ingredients.

Lemon Blueberry Muffins ... Amy Swartzentruber

½ c. butter, softened
1 c. sugar
2 eggs
½ c. milk
2 Tbsp. lemon juice
2 tsp. grated lemon peel
2 c. all-purpose flour
2 tsp. baking powder
dash of salt
2 c. blueberries, fresh or frozen

Glaze:

1½ c. powdered sugar
2 Tbsp. lemon juice
1 tsp. butter, melted
¼ tsp. vanilla extract

Cream butter and sugar in a large bowl until light and fluffy. Add eggs one at a time, beating well after each addition. Beat in the milk, lemon juice and lemon peel. Combine the flour, baking powder and salt; add to creamed mixture just until moistened. Fold in blueberries. Fill paper-lined muffin cups ¾ full. Bake at 400° for 25–30 minutes or until a toothpick inserted in muffin comes out clean. Cool for 5 minutes before removing from pan to a wire rack. Combine glaze ingredients. Drizzle over warm muffins.
Note: If using frozen blueberries, use without thawing to avoid discoloring the batter.
Yield: 24 muffins.

Pumpkin Apple Muffins .... Rachel Kanagy

½ c. vegetable oil
2 c. pumpkin
2 eggs
2 c. apples, peeled and diced
1 tsp. soda
½ tsp. salt
2 c. sugar
2½ c. flour

Topping:

2 Tbsp. flour
½ tsp. cinnamon
¼ c. sugar
1 Tbsp. butter

Combine oil, pumpkin and eggs. Stir in apples. In a separate bowl, mix remaining dry ingredients. Combine until moistened. Fill greased muffin cups ¾ full of batter. Sprinkle a generous teaspoon of topping onto each muffin. Bake at 350° for 20–25 minutes.
Yield: 20 muffins.

Yellow Squash Muffins .... Renae Weaver

2 c. yellow squash, cooked and mashed
2 eggs
1 c. butter, melted
1 c. sugar
3 c. flour
5 tsp. baking powder
1 tsp. salt
melted butter
cinnamon
sugar

Combine squash, eggs, and butter. Stir well; set aside. Combine dry ingredients in a large bowl. Make a well in center of mixture and add squash mixture to dry ingredients. Stir until blended. Spoon into lined muffin pan, filling ¾ full. Bake at 375° for 25 minutes. Brush with melted butter. Mix cinnamon and sugar and dip tops of muffins.

Note: These are very moist muffins.

Yield: 18 muffins.

Easy Pancakes .... Ruth Weaver

1½ c. all-purpose flour
3½ tsp. baking powder
1 tsp. salt
1 Tbsp. white sugar
1¼ c. milk
1 egg
3 Tbsp. butter, melted

Sift dry ingredients together then add the wet ingredients. Mix and let stand 5 minutes. Spoon about ¼ cup batter onto hot griddle for each pancake. Wait until bubbles form in the center and then flip. Cook on other side until golden brown, and then remove.

Yield: about 14 pancakes.

Oatmeal Pancake Mix ...... *Fannie Mae Kanagy*

Pancake Mix:
4 c. old fashioned oats
2 c. all-purpose flour
2 c. whole wheat flour
1 c. packed brown sugar
1 c. instant nonfat dry milk
3 Tbsp. baking powder
2 Tbsp. cinnamon
5 tsp. salt
½ tsp. cream of tartar

Pancakes:
2 eggs
⅓ c. vegetable oil
2 c. pancake mix
1 c. milk

Combine pancake mix ingredients and store in airtight container.
Yield: 10 cups mix.

To make pancakes: beat eggs in a large bowl. Gradually beat in oil. Alternately add pancake mix and milk to mixture. Blend well. Preheat and grease griddle. Pour ⅓ cup batter onto griddle. Cook until bubbles form around edges, turn and cook until done.
Yield: 10 servings.

Stuffed French Toast .... *Sheryl Kanagy*

16 slices bread

Filling:
1 (8 oz) pkg. cream cheese, softened
1 Tbsp. sugar
¼ tsp. cinnamon

Egg Mixture:
2 eggs, lightly beaten
¼ c. milk
1 tsp. vanilla

Syrup:
2 Tbsp. sugar
1 Tbsp. cornstarch
½ c. water
¼ c. pancake syrup
1½ c. frozen blueberries

Spread cream cheese on eight slices of bread; top with remaining eight slices. Dip into egg mixture and fry on a hot griddle until golden brown on both sides. Combine syrup ingredients and bring to a boil over medium heat. Simmer 5 minutes. Serve hot over stuffed toast.
Yield: 12 servings.

Waffles .... *Alta Miller*

3 c. flour
4 tsp. baking powder
1 tsp. salt
4 eggs, separated
⅔ c. butter, melted
2 c. milk

Mix dry ingredients. Add melted butter. Add milk gradually with beaten egg yolks. Beat egg whites till stiff, then fold into batter.
Note: For variation, add chopped nuts to batter.
Yield: 12 servings.

Baked Oatmeal .... *Esther Stoltzfus*

3 c. oatmeal
½ c. brown sugar
2 tsp. baking powder
1 tsp. salt
1 tsp. cinnamon
1 c. milk
2 eggs
½ c. butter, melted

Combine first five ingredients. Add remaining ingredients and stir. Bake in greased 9"x9" pan at 350° for 30 minutes. Serve with milk and peaches.
Note: This is Davalyan's favorite breakfast.
Yield: 5-6 servings.

Baked Oatmeal .... *Sheryl Kanagy*

¼ c. butter
¾ c. brown sugar
2 eggs
2 tsp. baking powder
1 tsp. salt
3 c. oatmeal
1 c. milk

Cream butter, brown sugar, and eggs. Add remaining ingredients and mix well. Pour batter into a greased 8"x8" pan and bake at 350° for 30 minutes. Serve warm with milk.
Note: For variation, add ½ teaspoon cinnamon, or sprinkle ¼ cup chocolate chips on top before baking.
Yield: 6 servings.

Granola .... *Alta Miller*

12 c. oatmeal
2 (16 oz.) jars wheat germ
2 (14 oz.) pkgs. coconut
3 c. chopped pecans

Sauce:
2 eggs, beaten
½ c. butter, melted
¾ c. oil
1 tsp. salt
¾ c. Karo or maple syrup
¾ c. honey
2 c. brown sugar

Mix together oatmeal, wheat germ, coconut and pecans. Mix the sauce ingredients, then pour over first mixture. Place on two large cookie sheets. Bake 1½ hours at 300°, stirring every 15 minutes. Store in plastic containers. Can be frozen.

Note: This recipe makes a large batch. You can freeze it to keep it fresh.

Granola .... *Gina Mast*

5 c. oatmeal
½ c. brown sugar
1 c. oat bran
½ c. chopped nuts
½ c. coconut
½ tsp. salt
½ c. honey
⅔ c. vegetable oil
2 Tbsp. water
1½ tsp. vanilla
½ tsp. maple flavoring

Combine oatmeal, brown sugar, bran, nuts and coconut. In separate bowl, combine remaining ingredients. Add to oatmeal mixture, stirring to coat well. Bake at 300° for 25–30 minutes, stirring every 5 minutes.

Granola .... Fannie Mae Kanagy

6 c. old fashioned oatmeal
2 c. coconut
1 c. pecans
1¼ c. brown sugar
1 c. butter or coconut oil
2 c. water
1½ tsp. salt
2 tsp. maple flavoring
1 tsp. vanilla
1 Tbsp. vinegar

Mix first four ingredients in large bowl. Melt butter or coconut oil in a separate pan. Add water, salt, maple flavoring, vanilla, and vinegar. Mix and combine with dry ingredients. Let soak for 4 hours. Spread on 2 cookie sheets or pans. Bake at 180° for 5 hours or until crispy.

Peanut Butter Granola .... Renae Weaver

5 c. quick oats
5 c. rolled oats
4 c. Rice Krispies
¾ c. wheat germ
1 c. coconut
1 c. brown sugar
¼ c. water
1½ c. vegetable oil
1 c. honey
½ tsp. salt
2 tsp. maple flavoring
½ tsp. vanilla
⅔ c. peanut butter

Combine first 6 ingredients in a large bowl. Cook together the water, oil, honey, salt, flavorings, and peanut butter until smooth. Pour over dry ingredients and mix. Place on 2 cookie sheets and bake at 300° for 30 minutes. Stir every 10 minutes.

Cheesy Egg Grits .... Rachel Kanagy

4 c. water
1 c. grits
1 tsp. salt
4 eggs, beaten
1½ c. shredded cheddar cheese
2 Tbsp. butter

Bring water to a boil. Add grits and salt. Bring back to a boil for 3-5 minutes. Stir in remaining ingredients and pour into an ungreased 9"x9" pan. Bake at 350° for 30 minutes.

Note: For variation, before baking, I like to stir in about ½ lb. of lil' smokies (cut in half) for a delicious flavor.

Yield: 6 servings.

Grits Casserole .... *Fannie Mae Kanagy*

6 c. water
1½ c. regular grits (not instant)
1 tsp. salt
4 c. shredded cheddar cheese
1 (4 oz.) can green chilies, chopped
3 eggs, beaten
¾ c. butter
1½ tsp. garlic or onion salt
dash of Tabasco sauce
1 (2.8 oz.) can French's Original french fried onions, crushed

In large saucepan, bring water to a boil. Add grits and salt then return to boil. Reduce heat and cook, uncovered, for 5 minutes, or until thickened. Remove from heat. Add cheese, chilies, eggs, butter, garlic salt and Tabasco. Pour into greased 9"x13" pan and bake 50 minutes at 350°. Sprinkle fried onions over top and bake 10 more minutes.

Yield: 12–16 servings.

Overnight Sausage and Grits ... *Renae Weaver*

3 c. cooked grits
1 lb. sausage, cooked and crumbled
2½ c. shredded cheddar cheese
3 eggs
1½ c. milk
3 Tbsp. butter, melted
¼ tsp. garlic powder

In a large bowl, mix grits, sausage, and cheese. Beat the eggs and milk; stir into grits. Add butter and garlic powder. Pour into a greased 9"x13" pan. Cover and chill 8 hours or overnight. Remove from the refrigerator 30 minutes before baking. Bake, uncovered, at 350° for 1 hour. Let stand 5 minutes before serving.

Yield: 10-12 servings.

Let's not confuse staunch steadfastness with stony stubbornness.

Breakfast Casserole .... *Tammy Yoder*

8 slices bread
¾ lb. sausage, ham, bacon or beef, fried
peppers (optional)
onions (optional)
6 eggs
2 c. milk
Velveeta cheese
1 can cream of mushroom soup
⅔ c. milk
2½ c. cornflakes
½ c. butter, melted

Cut bread in one inch cubes. Place in a 9"x13" pan. Next, layer your choice of meat and peppers and onions. Whip together eggs and 2 cups milk, pour over meat and bread. Top with slices of Velveeta cheese. Mix cream of mushroom soup and ⅔ cup milk, pour over Velveeta. Refrigerate overnight or 8 hours. Next morning, top with cornflakes and butter.
Yield: 8-10 servings.

Brunch Pizza Cups .... *Esther Stoltzfus*

1 tube biscuits
2-3 eggs, beaten
sausage or bacon, fried and crumbled
maple or pancake syrup
shredded cheese

Spray cupcake pan with cooking spray. Roll out biscuits to fit in cupcake pan. Fill about half full of egg. Add 1-2 teaspoon of pancake syrup and then meat. Bake at 350° till eggs are set or golden brown. Sprinkle some cheese on top and put back in oven till melted.

Easy Breakfast Pizza .... *Amy Swartzentruber*

½ tube crescent rolls
½ c. sausage crumbles
½ c. shredded potatoes or hash browns
onions to taste
2 eggs
¼ c. milk
½ c. shredded cheddar cheese
salt and pepper to taste

Press crescent rolls in greased 8"x8" pan. Mix milk with eggs and scramble. Top crescent roll with sausage crumbles, hash-browns, onions, eggs, and cheese. Bake at 350° for 20 minutes or until crust is golden brown.
Yield: 2-4 servings.

Egg Bake .... *Alta Miller*

26–30 oz. hash browns
6 Tbsp. vegetable oil
2½ c. shredded cheddar cheese
2½ c. meat of your choice
3 c. milk
7 eggs, beaten
2 tsp. salt
2 tsp. pepper
1 Tbsp. chopped onions

Mix hash browns and oil, then press on bottom of 9"x13" pan. Sprinkle cheese on top, then meat. Mix milk, eggs, salt, pepper, and onions. Pour over other ingredients. Bake 30–40 minutes at 425°.

Yield: 12-15 servings.

Hash Brown Bake .... *Susan Miller*

4 c. frozen hash browns
3 Tbsp. butter, divided
¼ tsp. salt
¼ tsp. pepper
1 med. onion, chopped
½ c. chopped green peppers
½ c. chopped fresh mushrooms
2 tsp. all-purpose flour
¾ c. diced ham, fully-cooked
3 eggs, beaten
½ c. milk
½ c. grated cheddar cheese

Brown hash browns in 2 tablespoons butter. Add salt and pepper. Press in a 10" pie pan. Sauté onions, green peppers and mushrooms in remaining butter. Sprinkle with flour. Spread over hash browns. Mix ham, eggs and milk and pour over first two layers. Bake at 350° for 25 minutes. Add cheese and bake 5 more minutes.

Yield: 6 servings.

Scrambled Egg Muffins .... *Susan Miller*

½ lb. bulk sausage
12 eggs
½ c. chopped onions
¼ c. chopped green peppers
½ tsp. salt
¼ tsp. pepper
¼ tsp. garlic powder
½ c. shredded cheddar cheese

Brown sausage; drain. Beat eggs, then add onions, green peppers, salt, pepper and garlic powder. Stir in sausage and cheese. Spoon by ⅓ cupfuls into greased muffin cups. Bake at 350° for 20–25 minutes or until knife inserted comes out clean.

Yield: 12 servings.

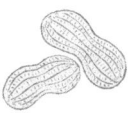

Southwest Sausage Bake .... *Elsie Yoder*

6 (10") flour tortillas
4 (4 oz.) cans green chilies, chopped and drained
1 lb. bulk pork sausage, cooked and drained
2 c. shredded Monterey Jack cheese
10 eggs
½ c. milk
½ tsp. salt
½ tsp. garlic salt
½ tsp. onion salt
½ tsp. pepper
½ tsp. ground cumin
paprika
2 medium tomatoes, sliced
sour cream
salsa

Cut flour tortillas into ½" strips. In a greased 9"x13" baking dish, layer half of the tortilla strips, chilies, sausage and cheese. Repeat layers. In a bowl; beat the eggs, milk and seasonings. Pour over cheese. Sprinkle with paprika. Cover and refrigerate overnight. Remove from refrigerator 30 minutes before baking. Bake, uncovered, at 350° for 50 minutes. Arrange tomato slices over the top. Bake 10–15 minutes longer or until a knife inserted near the center comes out clean. Let stand for 10 minutes before cutting. Serve with sour cream and salsa.
Yield: 12 servings.

Spinach Quiche .... *Alta Miller*

3 eggs, beaten
1 (10 oz.) pkg. frozen spinach, chopped
2 c. low-fat cottage cheese
3 Tbsp. shredded Swiss cheese
½ tsp. Dijon mustard
¼ tsp. instant minced onions
¼ tsp. dry mustard
¼ tsp. red pepper
⅛ tsp. salt

Thaw spinach and drain very well. Combine all ingredients and pour into a 9" unbaked pie crust. Bake at 350° until center is set.

Spinach Quiche .... *Valetta Yoder*

1 tube crescent rolls
Swiss cheese, sliced
1 box frozen spinach
meat of your choice
mushrooms (optional)
peppers (optional)
onions (optional)
8 eggs
1½ c. milk
1 tsp. salt
1 tsp. pepper

Line a greased 9"x13" pan with crescent rolls. Make a layer of sliced Swiss cheese. Drain spinach and layer on top of cheese. Sauté vegetables; add to pan. Next, make a layer of meat. Mix eggs with milk, salt and pepper. Pour over top. Cover loosely with foil. Bake at 350° for 1 hour.

Yield. 8 servings.

A Taste of Blackville

Recipe featured on previous page:
Poppy Seed Dressing *page 66*

Bean and Barley Salad .... Fern Weaver

¾ c. quick cooking barley
1 (16 oz.) can kidney beans
1 (15 oz.) can black beans
1 (11 oz.) can whole kernel corn
1 large sweet red pepper, chopped
½ c. chopped onions
⅓ c. fresh cilantro, minced, (optional)

Dressing:

¾ c. olive oil
⅓ c. vinegar
½ tsp. garlic powder
1½ tsp. chili powder
¾ tsp. salt
¾ tsp. ground cumin
¼ tsp. red pepper
¼ tsp. pepper

Prepare barley according to package directions. Put in large bowl. Drain and rinse beans and corn.
Mix dressing and pour over vegetables.
Note: This is also great as a dip for Tostito chips.
Yield: 12 (¾ cup) servings.

BLT Salad .... Renae Weaver

8 c. chopped lettuce
2 large tomatoes, chopped
10 strips bacon, fried and crumbled
1 c. shredded cheddar cheese
2 hard-boiled eggs, sliced

Dressing:

½ c. mayonnaise
¼ c. barbecue sauce
2 Tbsp. finely chopped onion
1 Tbsp. lemon juice
¼ tsp. pepper

Place lettuce on a large serving platter. Sprinkle with tomatoes, bacon, and cheese. Garnish with eggs. Combine dressing ingredients. Refrigerate until ready to serve. Drizzle with dressing just before serving.
Yield: 8-10 servings.

Broccoli Cauliflower Salad..... *Esther Stoltzfus*

1 head cauliflower
1 small head of broccoli
cheese
bacon bits

Dressing:

1 c. mayonnaise
⅓ c. sugar
¼–½ tsp. dry mustard
pinch of salt
milk

Cut up broccoli and cauliflower.
Dressing: Mix together mayon--naise, sugar, mustard, salt and a little milk. Stir dressing into broccoli and cauliflower when ready to eat. Top with shredded cheese and bacon bits if desired.

Chicken and Black Bean Salad. *Tammy Yoder*

6 c. romaine lettuce, torn
1 can black beans,
  rinsed and drained
1 can whole kernel
  corn, drained
1 med. red bell pepper, diced
⅓ c. chopped green onions
1½ c. chicken, cooked
  or grilled

Dressing:

⅓ c. vegetable oil
2 Tbsp. lime juice
2 Tbsp. fresh cilantro
1½ tsp. sugar
½ tsp. chili powder
½ tsp. salt (optional)
¼ tsp. pepper
1 garlic clove, minced

On a serving platter layer lettuce, beans, corn, red peppers, onions and chicken.
  In a separate bowl combine dressing ingredients. Drizzle over salad and serve immediately. Makes a delicious, light, summer meal.

Chinese Chicken Salad .... *Susan Miller*

1 head lettuce
6 oz. chow mein noodles
4 oz. sliced almonds
1 c. chicken,
    cooked and cubed
onion (optional)

Dressing:

½ c. sugar
¼ c. vinegar
½ c. vegetable oil
2 tsp. salt
½ tsp. pepper
1 tsp. poppy seeds

Mix together salad ingredients. *Dressing:* bring sugar and vinegar to boil till sugar is dissolved. Add oil, salt, pepper and poppy seeds. Mix well. Cool. Add to salad just before serving.
Yield: 10-12 servings.

Cole Slaw .... *Fannie Mae Kanagy*

1 large head cabbage
    chopped or shredded
1 carrot, grated

Dressing:

2 c. mayonnaise
1 c. sugar
1 tsp. salt
½ tsp. paprika
½ tsp. white pepper
½ tsp. dry mustard
¼ c. chopped onions
1 Tbsp. vinegar

Stir or blend dressing ingredients together. Mix dressing with cabbage and carrots. Dressing will keep in refrigerator for several weeks.
Yield: 10-12 servings.

Festive Tossed Salad .... *Tammy Yoder*

1 c. pecans, coarsely chopped
2 Tbsp. butter
¼ c. sugar
½ tsp. pepper
¼ tsp. salt
12 c. romaine lettuce, torn
¾ c. dried cranberries
4 oz. Feta cheese, crumbled
red onion, sliced

Dressing:

½ c. red wine vinegar
½ c. vegetable oil
1 tsp. parsley flakes
1 garlic clove
⅔ c. sugar
½ tsp. oregano
⅛ tsp. salt
⅛ tsp. pepper

In a skillet, stir pecans in butter until lightly toasted. Remove from heat. Stir in sugar, pepper and salt. In a serving bowl; toss lettuce, cranberries, cheese, onions and pecans.
Dressing: Put all ingredients in a blender and mix. Pour desired amount over salad. Toss and serve immediately.
Yield: 12 servings.

Marinated Tomato Salad ...... *Susanna Kanagy*

8 med. tomatoes, sliced
¼ c. minced fresh parsley
¼ c. olive or vegetable oil
2 Tbsp. cider or red wine vinegar
2 tsp. mustard
1 garlic clove, minced
1 tsp. sugar
1 tsp. salt

Arrange tomato slices in serving bowl or platter. Sprinkle with parsley. Combine remaining ingredients and drizzle over tomatoes. Cover and refrigerate 30 minutes before serving.
Note: I like to keep a jar of this dressing in the refrigerator during tomato season to drizzle over fresh garden tomatoes.
Yield: 12 servings.

Broccoli and Pasta Salad........... *Elsie Yoder*

½ lb. bow-tie pasta, prepared
1 lb. fresh broccoli
2 c. red grapes, halved
8 bacon slices, cooked and crumbled
1 c. pecans, chopped and toasted

Dressing:
1 c. mayonnaise
⅓ c. sugar
⅓ c. diced red onions
⅓ c. red wine vinegar
1 tsp. salt

Whisk dressing ingredients together in a large bowl, add broccoli, cooked pasta, and grapes. Stir to coat. Cover and chill 3 hours. Just before serving, stir bacon and pecans into salad.

Yield: 6-8 servings.

Pasta Salad........................... *Gina Mast*

2 lb. pasta, cooked and drained
16 oz. Italian dressing
Italian salad seasoning to taste
green peppers, diced
tomatoes, diced
onion, diced
pepperoni
cheddar cheese, cubed
green and black olives, sliced

Mix all ingredients together. Best results if left sitting overnight.

Yield: 1 fix and mix bowl.

Pasta Salad ...... *Sheryl Kanagy*

1 lb. pasta, cooked
1 med. green pepper, diced
1 sm. onion, diced
1 cucumber, diced
1 tomato diced
30 sliced black olives
¾ c. pepperoni, cubed

Dressing:

2½ Tbsp. McCormick
　Salad Supreme
1 pkg. Good Seasons dry
　Italian dressing mix
16 oz. Viva Italian dressing
2 Tbsp. sour cream (optional)
salt and sugar to taste

Prepare salad ingredients and place in large bowl.
　Dressing: Combine all ingredients. Pour dressing mixture over pasta and stir gently.

Potato Salad ...... *Sheryl Kanagy*

6 c. potatoes, cooked
　and shredded
5 eggs, hard-boiled
　and shredded
¼ c. diced onions
1 c. chopped celery

Dressing:

1½ c. salad dressing
1½ tsp. mustard
2 tsp. vinegar
½ c. sugar
1½ tsp. salt

Prepare first four ingredients and place in a large bowl. Combine the dressing ingredients and pour over potato mixture. Stir gently. Refrigerate until ready to serve.
　Note: Three batches fill a fix and mix bowl and serves 50 people.
　Yield: 15 servings.

Potato Salad .... *Lill Stoltzfus*

8 potatoes
3 eggs, hard-boiled and diced

Dressing:
¾ c. mayonnaise
¾ Tbsp. mustard
1 Tbsp. vinegar
1 Tbsp. salt
½ c. sugar
2 Tbsp. milk
½ sm. onion

Cook, peel, cool, and dice potatoes.
Dressing: Mix ingredients in blender. Mix with potatoes and eggs.
Note: Best if made 1 day ahead.
Yield: 8-10 servings.

Ramen Noodle Salad .... *Gina Mast*

2 lb. broccoli, cut up
1 c. chopped onions,
1 c. diced tomatoes,
2 c. sunflower seeds
2 c. slivered almonds
2–3 pkg. Ramen noodles

Mix broccoli, onions, and tomatoes. In separate bowl, combine dressing ingredients. Wait to add sunflower seeds, almonds, noodles and dressing until just before serving.

Dressing:
1 c. vegetable oil
1 c. sugar
⅔ c. vinegar
seasonings from noodle pkg.

Southwest Chicken Salad .... Valetta Yoder

onions
chicken breasts
taco seasoning
lettuce
black beans
cheddar cheese
taco chips

Dressing:

2 c. sour cream
2 c. salsa

Sauté onions, add chicken. Continue to sauté until chicken is no longer pink. Add taco seasoning to taste. Layer lettuce, black beans, cheese and chips on platter. Top with chicken and onions. Mix dressing ingredients together and pour over salad. Makes a delicious summer evening meal.

Cottage Cheese and Pineapple Salad ...
Katie E. Stoltzfus

3 oz. lemon or lime Jell-O
1 c. hot water
1 c. pineapple juice
1 c. crushed pineapple, drained
1 c. cottage cheese
½ c. chopped nuts
¼ tsp. salt
green and red pepper strips

Dissolve Jell-O in hot water and add pineapple juice. Chill until liquid begins to congeal. Combine pineapple, cheese, nuts, and salt and fold into Jell-O mixture. Pour into mold and chill until firm. Unmold on lettuce and garnish with mayonnaise and strips of pepper.
Yield: 6 servings.

Cottage Cheese Jello Salad .... Rachel Kanagy

3 c. boiling water
2 c. lime Jell-O
4 c. cold water
24 oz. cottage cheese
1 can crushed pineapple with juice

Stir Jell-O into boiling water until dissolved. Add remaining ingredients and pour into serving bowl. Chill until beginning to congeal, then stir and chill until firm.
Note: This is a recipe from my Grandma Shank. Our family had it for many, many Sunday lunches!
Yield: 15-20 servings.

Cranberry Salad .... *Rachel Kanagy*

6 oz. strawberry Jell-O
2 c. boiling water
1 c. cold water
2 large apples, peeled and shredded
1½ c. whole cranberries
12 oz. mandarin oranges, drained
½ c. sugar
cottage cheese, (optional)

Dissolve Jell-O in boiling water. Add cold water and apples. Chop cranberries into pieces. Put in separate bowl. Add oranges. Sprinkle sugar over fruit and let soak 5 minutes. Combine fruit with Jell-O. Pour into a Jell-O mold or serving bowl, and chill until beginning to set. Stir and chill thoroughly. Serve with cottage cheese.
Note: This is a family Thanksgiving and Christmas tradition!
Yield: 12 servings.

Cranberry Salad .... *Alta Miller*

2 lg. boxes cherry Jell-O
2 cans pineapple, drained (use liquid with Jell-O)
1 bag cranberries
2 c. sugar
1½ Tbsp. lemon juice
2 cans mandarin oranges, cut up
2 c. chopped celery
1 c. chopped nuts

Mix Jell-O according to pkg. directions. Drained pineapple juice can be used for some of the liquid. Blend cranberries coarsely in blender with one cup Jell-O. Mix with remaining Jell-O and refrigerate till partially set. Add sugar and lemon juice. Let set. Add cut up oranges, celery and nuts to Jell-O. Stir, then put in desired containers and let it totally set up.
Note: I omit the 2 cups sugar and we like it very well!
Yield: 24 servings.

Dreamsicle Jell-O Salad .... *Renae Weaver*

2–6 oz. boxes strawberry Jell-O
1 c. sugar
4 c. boiling water
2 c. ice and water
16 oz. cream cheese, softened
4 c. whipped cream
fresh strawberries to garnish

Dissolve sugar and Jell-O in boiling water. Add ice and water. Let sit until syrupy. Beat cream cheese until smooth. Add whipped cream. Slowly pour in Jell-O mixture and mix well. Pour into a container that holds at least three quart. Refrigerate until set. Garnish with fresh strawberries and serve.
Yield: 12 servings.

Easy Finger Jell-O .... *Susanna Kanagy*

4 pkg. Jell-O, any flavor
2½ c. boiling water

Stir boiling water into Jell-O until dissolved. Pour into 9"x13" pan and refrigerate until set. Cut in squares or use cookie cutters to cut out fun shapes.

Finger Jell-O .... *Esther Stoltzfus*

2 env. Knox gelatin
3 (4 serving size) boxes Jell-O
4 c. boiling water

In a large bowl combine Knox gelatin and Jell-O. Add boiling water and stir until completely dissolved. Pour in a 9"x13" pan and chill. Cut in squares.

Cole Slaw Dressing .... *Lill Stoltzfus*

½ onion
¾ c. vinegar
2 c. sugar
2 c. mayonnaise
2 Tbsp. mustard
2 tsp. salt
1 tsp. celery salt
¼ tsp. pepper
¼ tsp. garlic powder

Put onion and vinegar in blender or food processor. Chop until onion is very fine. Add remaining ingredients and blend well.
Note: Dressing stays good in refrigerator for several weeks. This recipe was used by Martha Schrock.
Yield: enough dressing for 2 heads of cabbage.

French Dressing .... *Sheryl Kanagy*

2 c. mayonnaise
1½ c. sugar
¼ c. vinegar
½ c. ketchup
2 tsp. mustard
2 tsp. paprika
½ tsp. salt
½ c. vegetable oil
4 tsp. water

Put all ingredients in blender and blend until thoroughly mixed.

Honey Bacon Dressing .... *Susan Miller*

2 bacon strips, cooked and crumbled
½ c. honey
½ c. vinegar
⅓ c. vegetable or olive oil
1 tsp. mustard
1 tsp. lemon juice
1 tsp. salt

Whisk all ingredients together. Delicious on spinach salad.
Yield: approximately 1½ cups.

Italian Dressing .... *Glenda Weaver*

¼ c. lemon juice
¼ c. vinegar
¾ c. olive oil
1 tsp. honey (optional)
½ tsp. garlic powder
½ tsp. onion powder
1 tsp. salt
½ tsp. dry mustard
½ tsp. oregano
½ tsp. basil
¼ tsp. paprika
½ tsp. kelp (optional)

Put everything in blender and mix well.

Poppy Seed Dressing .... *Esther Stoltzfus*

½ c. vegetable oil
¾ c. vinegar
½ c. sugar
½ tsp. poppy seeds
1 Tbsp. grated onion
1 tsp. dry mustard
1 tsp. salt

Blend together. Chill. Delicious with chopped cucumbers and tomatoes.
   Note: For oil, I use olive oil.

Sweet and Sour Dressing .... *Sheryl Kanagy*

1 c. sugar
1 c. vegetable oil
1 Tbsp. salad dressing
2 tsp. mustard
1 med. onion, chopped
¼ c. water
¼ c. vinegar
1 tsp. salt
¼ tsp. pepper
1 tsp. celery seed

Mix all ingredients together in blender.
   Yield: approximately 3 cups.

Sweet and Sour Dressing .... *Fern Weaver*

1 sm. onion
1 c. vegetable oil
1 Tbsp. mustard
1 c. sugar
1 tsp. salt
½ tsp. pepper
1 tsp. celery salt
⅓ c. vinegar
2 Tbsp. mayonnaise

Mix all together in blender. Serve on salads or as a dipping sauce for chicken.

My job is to increase the number of happiness moments in the lives of all the people with whom I come in contact.

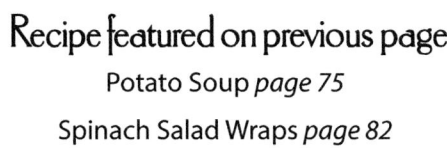

Recipe featured on previous page:
Potato Soup *page 75*
Spinach Salad Wraps *page 82*

Catfish Stew .... *Lill Stoltzfus*

2 med. sized catfish
4 bacon strips
1 lg. onion,
  finely chopped
3 stalks celery
6 potatoes, cubed
1 pt. canned tomatoes
Worcestershire sauce
½ c. butter
1 sm. can evaporated milk
1 can cream of mushroom
  soup (optional)
1 can tomato paste
  (optional)
Hot sauce

Boil catfish in kettle with water. Boil until soft and able to pick off from bones. Reserve water. While fish are boiling, fry bacon and remove from pan; add onions and celery and sauté. Add cubed potatoes and enough reserved water to cover. After soft, mash with potato masher. Add catfish, tomatoes and a few dashes of Worcestershire sauce. Continue to simmer, adding water left from cooking catfish. Slowly simmer for a least 2 hours. In the last half hour of cooking, add butter, evaporated milk, mushroom soup and tomato paste. Serve with hot sauce.

Note: I got this recipe from Southern neighbors. It is one of Alvin's favorite dishes.

Yield: 6 servings.

Chili Soup .... *Gina Mast*

1 lb. hamburger
2 med. onions, chopped
1 qt. tomato juice
¼ tsp. pepper
2 tsp. salt
1 tsp. chili powder
1 can pork and beans
Brown sugar
  to taste (optional)
Barbecue sauce
  to taste (optional)

Fry onion and hamburger until meat is no longer pink. Mix together all ingredients and simmer about 15 minutes. Add water to obtain desired consistency.

Chili Soup .... *Ruth Weaver*

1 lb. ground beef
1 sm. onion, chopped
2 Tbsp. butter
½ c. flour
½ c. brown sugar
2 c. water
1 (15 oz.) can kidney beans or pork and beans
chili seasoning
salt and pepper to taste
1 qt. tomato juice

Brown beef and onion in butter in medium kettle. Add flour and sugar and brown just a little. Slowly stir in water. Add beans, seasonings and tomato juice. Simmer for 15 minutes.
Yield: 6-8 servings.

Clam Chowder .... *Alta Miller*

1 c. chopped onions
1 c. chopped celery
4 c. diced potatoes
4 (7 oz.) cans minced clams
4 slices bacon
¼ c. butter
½ c. flour
2 qt. milk
salt and pepper
2 c. frozen corn
16 oz. chicken broth

Drain clams and save juice. Cook onions, celery and potatoes in clam juice till tender. In a large kettle fry bacon till crisp. Remove bacon and crumble. Leave bacon grease in kettle and add butter till melted. Add flour and stir till bubbly. Gradually add milk and stir till it thickens. Add clams, bacon, corn, salt, pepper, chicken broth, and vegetables. Stir and bring almost to a boil.
Note: Prepare a day ahead so flavor can blend. It is also delicious to add 1 pound of small raw or cooked, peeled shrimp.
Yield: 5 quarts or 12 servings.

Creamy White Chili .... *Tammy Yoder*

1 lb. chicken breast, cubed
1 med. onion, chopped
1½ tsp. garlic powder
1 Tbsp. vegetable oil
1 (15 oz.) can Northern beans, drained and rinsed
1 (4 oz.) can green chilies
2 c. chicken broth
1 tsp. salt
½ tsp. pepper
¼ tsp. cayenne pepper
¼ tsp. cumin
1 tsp. oregano
1 c. sour cream
½ c. whipping cream

Sauté chicken, onion and garlic powder in oil. Add next eight ingredients. Bring to boil and simmer, uncovered for 30 minutes. Add sour cream and whipping cream. Heat through but do not boil.

Yield: approximately 7 servings.

Creamy Wild Rice Soup .... *Susan Miller*

1 c. wild rice, uncooked
½ c. chopped onions
¾ c. chopped carrots
¾ c. butter
⅔ c. flour
5 c. chicken or ham broth
½ tsp. pepper
1 c. diced ham
1 c. milk

Cook rice according to package directions. Sauté onion and carrot in butter for 2 minutes. Stir in flour. Gradually add broth and bring to boil, stirring until thickened. Add pepper, ham and rice. Simmer 5 minutes, than add milk and heat through.

Yield: 6-8 servings.

If you have something unpleasant to do today, do it first and do it fast.

Ham Cheddar Chowder .... *Rachel Kanagy*

2 c. water or chicken broth
1 c. potatoes, peeled and diced
¼ c. chopped celery
½ c. chopped carrots
¼ c. chopped onions
1 c. cooked ham, diced
¼ c. butter
¼ c. flour
2 c. milk
2 c. shredded cheddar cheese
1½ tsp. salt
½ tsp. pepper

Boil water and vegetables for 15 minutes or until vegetables are soft. Add ham. In a separate saucepan, melt butter. Add flour and mix well. Whisk in milk. Bring to a boil. Remove from heat and add cheese, salt, and pepper.
Yield: 6-8 servings.

Mexican Shrimp Bisque ..... *Amy Swartzentruber*

½ c. chopped onions
2 cloves garlic, minced
1 Tbsp. olive oil
1 Tbsp. all-purpose flour
1 c. water
½ c. heavy whipping cream
1 Tbsp. chili powder
2 tsp. chicken bouillon granules
½ tsp. ground cumin
½ tsp. ground coriander
½ lb. uncooked med. shrimp, peeled and deveined
½ c. sour cream
fresh cilantro and cubed avocado, (optional)

In a large saucepan, sauté onion and garlic in oil until tender. Stir in flour until blended. Stir in the water, cream, chili powder, bouillon, cumin and coriander; bring to a boil. Reduce heat, cover and simmer for 5 minutes. Cut shrimp into bite-sized pieces, add to soup. Simmer 5 minutes longer or until shrimp turn pink. Gradually stir ½ cup hot soup into sour cream, return all to pan. Stir constantly. Heat through, but do not boil. Garnish with cilantro and avocado if desired.
Yield: 2-4 servings.

Mushroom Sausage Pizza Soup — *Valetta Yoder*

1 lb. Italian turkey sausage
2 onions, chopped
10 oz. fresh mushrooms
6 garlic cloves, minced
1 large zucchini
2 (15 oz.) cans diced tomatoes
3 c. chicken broth
1 c. water
1 (8 oz.) can tomato sauce
3 Tbsp. tomato paste
1 Tbsp. Italian seasoning
2 tsp. basil
½ tsp. pepper
¼ tsp. red pepper flakes
Parmesan cheese
Mozzarella cheese

Crumble sausage and add onions and mushrooms. Cook and stir over medium heat until meat is no longer pink. Add garlic and zucchini; cook and stir 2 minutes longer. Add tomatoes, broth, water, and tomato sauce. Reduce heat and add tomato paste. Simmer 15 minutes and then add spices and simmer 15 more minutes. Ladle into bowls and sprinkle with Parmesan and Mozzarella cheese.

Potato Soup .... *Glenda Weaver*

½ c. chopped onions
2 c. cubed potatoes
1 c. water
1½ c. milk
½ tsp. salt
½ tsp. pepper
1 can cream of chicken soup
1 c. sour cream
Velveeta cheese
bacon

Cook onions and potatoes until soft. Mix together water, milk, salt, pepper and cream of chicken soup. Add to potatoes. Bring to a boil and simmer for 30 minutes. Add sour cream and cheese just before serving. Sprinkle with bacon.

Yield: 5 servings.

Taco Soup .... *Glenda Weaver*

1½ lbs. hamburger
salt and pepper to taste
1 sm. onion, chopped
3 Tbsp. flour
1 pkg. taco seasoning
1 can refried beans
1½ qt. tomato juice
⅔ c. brown sugar
corn chips
shredded cheese
sour cream

Fry hamburger and onion, drain. Pour hamburger in a large kettle and season with salt and pepper. Add flour, taco seasoning, beans, brown sugar and tomato juice. Simmer 30 minutes over low heat. Serve with corn chips, cheese, and sour cream.

Three Ingredients Soup .... *Maryglenn Brown*

1 lb. egg noodles
2 qt. tomatoes, chunked
2 qt. raw or whole milk
salt and pepper

Cook noodles to your taste. Heat milk and tomatoes in kettle. Add cooked noodles. Season with salt and pepper to taste.
Note: 2% milk will separate and curdle.
Yield: 6 servings.

Barbecue Sandwiches .... *Fern Weaver*

5 lb. chicken, cooked
  and deboned
2 c. barbecue sauce (of your
  choice, we like Baby Rays)
1 Tbsp. brown sugar
½ tsp. salt
½ tsp. onion powder

Put everything in crockpot on medium heat until well heated. Serve on mayonnaise bread or buns.
Note: These are very good with cold milk and fruit soup, on a warm summer evening.

Barbecued Burgers .... *Gina Mast*

Sauce:
- 1 c. ketchup
- ½ c. packed brown sugar
- ⅓ c. sugar
- ¼ c. honey
- ¼ c. molasses
- 2 tsp. mustard
- 1½ tsp. Worcestershire sauce
- ¼ tsp. salt
- ¼ tsp. liquid smoke
- ⅛ tsp. pepper

Burgers:
- 1 egg, lightly beaten
- ⅓ c. quick oats
- ¼ tsp. onion salt
- ¼ tsp. garlic salt
- ¼ tsp. pepper
- ⅛ tsp. salt
- 1½ lb. ground beef
- 6 hamburger buns
- toppings of your choice

Sauce: In small saucepan, combine all ingredients. Bring to a boil. Remove from the heat. Set aside 1 cup barbecue sauce to serve with burgers.

Burgers: In a large bowl combine the egg, oats, ¼ cup of the remaining barbecue sauce, onion salt, garlic salt, pepper and salt. Crumble beef over mixture and mix well. Shape into 6 patties. Grill, covered, over medium heat for 6–8 minutes on each side or until a meat thermometer reads 160°. Baste with ½ cup barbecue sauce during the last 5 minutes. Serve burgers on buns with toppings of your choice and the reserved barbecue sauce.

Yield: 6 servings.

Beefy Bunwiches....................*Renae Weaver*

Buns:

1 c. milk
1 tsp. salt
2 tsp. sugar
1 Tbsp. yeast
½ c. warm water
4 c. bread flour

Filling:

1 lb. ground beef, browned
1 sm. onion, chopped
¾ c. oatmeal
¼ head cabbage, shredded
3 c. shredded cheddar cheese
1 tsp. salt
½ tsp. oregano
½ tsp. basil
½ tsp. chili powder

Scald milk, add salt and sugar. Cool to lukewarm. Dissolve yeast in warm water; add to cooled milk. Add flour and knead into a smooth dough. Cover and let rise for 1 hour. Combine all filling ingredients. Divide dough into 12 pieces. Roll each piece into a 6" square. Top with ½ cup filling. Bring corners together and pinch shut. Place seam side down on a greased cookie sheet. Let rise 25 minutes. Bake at 350° for 25–30 minutes. Serve with ketchup.
Yield: 12 sandwiches.

Cheddar and Bacon Burgers..............
Amy Swartzentruber

½ c. shredded cheddar cheese
½ c. crumbled, cooked bacon
1 env. onion soup mix
2 lb. ground beef

Combine cheese, bacon, and soup mix in large bowl. Crumble beef over mixture and mix well. Shape into 8 patties. Grill burgers, covered, over medium heat or broil 4" from the heat for 5–7 minutes on both sides, until done to your liking.
Yield: 6 servings.

Chicken Salad .... *Alta Miller*

4 c. chicken, cooked
1 c. chopped celery
1 c. grapes, halved
1 c. mayo
½ c. sour cream
¼ c. chopped onions
4 oz. almonds, sliced or slivered
1 Tbsp. sugar
¼ tsp. paprika
¼ tsp. onion salt
¼ tsp. celery salt
¼ tsp. dry mustard
½ tsp. mustard
½ tsp. salt
½ tsp. pepper

Mix together all ingredients except chicken. Fold in chicken last. Great for sandwiches or with crackers.

Hot Chicken Salad .... *Valetta Yoder*

6 slices bread
2½ c. chicken, cooked and diced
½ c. chopped onions
½ c. chopped peppers
½ c. chopped celery
½ c. salad dressing
¾ tsp. salt
dash of pepper
2 eggs
1 c. milk
1 can cream of mushroom soup
½ c. grated cheese
parsley

Cube 2 slices of bread, place in a greased 8" x 8" x 2" baking dish. Combine chicken, vegetables, salad dressing, salt, and pepper. Spoon over bread cubes. Trim crust and cube remaining 4 slices and place on top of chicken mixture. Beat eggs into milk and pour over top of bread. Cover dish and chill at least 1 hour or overnight before baking. Spoon undiluted mushroom soup over top of bread. Bake at 350° for 45 minutes. Sprinkle cheese over top and garnish with parsley. Bake 15 more minutes.

Coney Sauce - Chili for Hot Dogs
Fern Weaver

1 c. chopped onions
1 c. chopped celery
2 lb. hamburger
salt
pepper
1 qt. ketchup
2 c. stewed tomatoes
¼ c. brown sugar
¼ c. cornstarch

Brown hamburger and onion together. Put in crockpot. Stir cornstarch in a little water, then add the rest of the ingredients. Cook slowly for 2 hours.

Note: We have lots of good memories of how good this tastes on hot dogs at The Horse Farmer's Gathering.

Grilled Cheese Sandwiches
Tammy Yoder

homemade bread
mayonnaise
shredded cheddar cheese
shredded mozzarella cheese
Feta cheese
basil
oregano
parsley flakes
Italian seasoning

Spread mayonnaise on bread. Top with cheeses and sprinkle with seasonings. Butter outsides of sandwiches and grill until golden brown.

Note: Delicious served with fried tomatoes and grits.

Pizza Sandwiches
Renae Weaver

2 c. shredded mozzarella cheese
2 c. shredded cheddar cheese
2 c. chopped pepperoni
2 lb. sausage, fried
1½ c. mayonnaise
1 c. pizza sauce
2 tsp. garlic powder

Mix all ingredients. Spread on English muffins or sandwich buns. Bake at 350° for 10–15 minutes.

Yield: 15 opened faced sandwiches.

Poppy Seed Sandwiches .... *Tammy Yoder*

2 pkg. King's Hawaiian sweet rolls
ham, sliced
Swiss cheese, sliced

Sauce:

½ c. butter
2 Tbsp. poppy seed
⅓ c. brown sugar
2 Tbsp. Worcestershire sauce
2 Tbsp. mustard

In a saucepan combine sauce ingredients and boil 2 minutes. In a pan, layer bottom half of rolls. Pour 1 teaspoon sauce over each bottom half. Layer on meat and cheese. Put on top half of bun. Pour rest of the sauce over the sandwiches. Bake covered, at 350° for 10 minutes. Uncover and bake 5–10 minutes longer.

Sloppy Joes - large recipe .... *Fannie Mae Kanagy*

14 lb. hamburger
3 c. chopped onions
6¾ c. quick oats
9 c. canned milk or top milk
4½ c. water
4½ c. chopped celery
9 c. ketchup
2 c. sugar (scant)
9 Tbsp. Worcestershire sauce
3 Tbsp. salt
1¼ c. vinegar

Brown hamburger and onions. Mix everything and bake at 300° for 1½ hours.
Yield: 100 servings.

Sloppy Joes .... *Rachel Kanagy*

2 lb. ground beef
1 med. onion, chopped
2 c. ketchup
2 Tbsp. mustard
¼ c. vinegar
¾ c. brown sugar
1 Tbsp. Worcestershire sauce
2 tsp. salt
2–4 Tbsp. oatmeal (if desired)

Fry beef and onion together. Drain off grease. Add remaining ingredients except oatmeal and simmer 5–10 minutes. Add several tablespoons of oatmeal if meat is too saucy. This will thicken it slightly so the bread will not become so soggy. Serve on bread or hamburger rolls.
Yield: 8 servings.

Spinach Salad Wraps .... *Amy Swartzentruber*

Dressing:
5 Tbsp. red wine vinegar
¼ c. sour cream
2 Tbsp. sugar
2 tsp. fresh parsley, snipped
1 tsp. salt
2 cloves garlic, minced
½ tsp. dry mustard
1 tsp. olive oil

1 (5 oz.) pkg. fresh baby spinach
6 (10") flour tortillas
6 slices mozzarella cheese, torn in half
8 oz. fresh mushrooms, sliced
12 slices bacon, crisp-cooked and drained
½ c. thinly sliced red onion
3 hard-boiled eggs, sliced

Dressing: In a small bowl whisk together all ingredients until combined. Set dressing aside. Divide spinach among flour tortillas. Top with cheese mushrooms, bacon, red onion, and sliced eggs. Drizzle with dressing. Roll up tortillas. If necessary, secure with toothpicks.
Yield: 6 servings.

Stromboli .... *Susanna Kanagy*

1 loaf frozen bread dough, thawed
2 eggs, separated
1 Tbsp. Parmesan cheese
1 tsp. parsley flakes
½ tsp. garlic powder
1 tsp. oregano
¼ tsp. pepper
2 Tbsp. vegetable oil
½ lb. pepperoni, sliced
12 oz. mozzarella cheese
pizza sauce, warmed

Roll out bread dough in a 12"x15" rectangle. Separate eggs, reserving whites. Combine egg yolks, Parmesan cheese, parsley, garlic powder, oregano, pepper and oil. Brush over bread dough. Layer with pepperoni. Sprinkle with mozzarella cheese. Roll up starting with long end. Pinch ends to seal. Place on greased baking sheet. Brush with reserved egg whites. Bake at 350° for 40–50 minutes. Serve with pizza sauce.
Note: Optional—Add mushrooms, peppers or sausage to the filling.
Yield: 6-8 servings.

Turkey Sandwiches . . . . *Lill Stoltzfus*

1 c. turkey, cut in chunks
¼ c. butter, melted
⅔ c. sour cream
2 Tbsp. chopped onions
1 Tbsp. parsley
French bread
Swiss cheese

Mix turkey, butter, sour cream, onions, and parsley together. Put on slices of French bread, sprinkle Swiss cheese on top. Broil for 5 minutes or till cheese melts.

Note: May substitute ham or chicken for turkey.

Yield: 4 servings.

God cannot forget you when you are as close to Him as the palms of His hands.

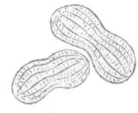

A Taste of Blackville

Meats & Main Dishes

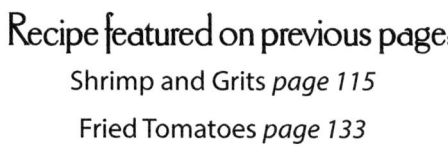

Recipe featured on previous page:
Shrimp and Grits *page 115*
Fried Tomatoes *page 133*

Alice Springs Chicken
Lori Miller

1 c. honey
1 c. Dijon or Poupon mustard
5–6 boneless skinless chicken breast
fresh mushrooms, sliced
grated cheese

Marinate chicken for 2–3 hours. Grill. Sauté mushrooms. After chicken is done top with mushrooms and grated cheese. Place in oven till cheese is melted.
Yield: 6 servings.

Baked Chicken in Mushroom Gravy
Glenda Weaver

3 Tbsp. melted butter
6 chicken breast
2 cans cream of mushroom soup
8 oz. cream cheese
½ c. bacon, fried and crumbled

Pour melted butter in 9"x13" pan. Place chicken breast in pan and add mixed soup and cream cheese. Sprinkle bacon on top. Cover and bake at 350° for 1 hour.
Yield: 5 servings.

We may live without poetry, music and art;
We may live without conscience, and live without heart;
We may live without friends, we may live without books,
But civilized man cannot live without cooks.
-Owen Meredith-

Belizean Rice and Beans with Ricardo Chicken
.... *Fannie Mae Kanagy and Sheryl Kanagy*

Rice & Beans:
1 c. dried kidney beans
2 Tbsp. chopped onions
1½ Tbsp. coconut oil or butter
2 tsp. salt
½ tsp. garlic powder
¼ tsp. pepper
2 c. rice, uncooked
3¼ c. water

Cook beans until soft. Fry onions in oil, then add beans, salt, seasonings, and water. Heat then add rice. Bring to a boil, and turn on low for 45 minutes, stirring several times. Let set for 1 hour or more. Serve with Ricardo chicken and gravy.
Yield: 6-8 servings.

Ricardo Chicken:
20 pieces chicken or 2 whole chickens, cut up
2 Tbsp. Ricardo
¼ c. water, scant
2 Tbsp. vinegar
1 Tbsp. Worcestershire sauce
1 Tbsp. pepper
2 tsp. salt
1 tsp. seasoned salt
1 tsp. chicken flavored bouillon
½ tsp. garlic powder
dash of Accent, (optional)
1 lg. onion, chopped
½ of a green pepper, chopped

Remove skin from chicken. Dissolve Ricardo in water, then add remaining ingredients, except for onion and green peppers. Dip each piece of chicken in Ricardo marinade and place in medium bowl. Pour any leftover marinade over chicken. Cover tightly and refrigerate 12-24 hours. When ready to bake, place chicken in medium roaster. Add chopped onions and green peppers and a little water (or any remaining Ricardo marinade). Cover and bake at 350° for 1½ hours. Serve the marinade sauce as a gravy for the rice and beans.
Yield: 12 servings.

Caprese Chicken with Bacon .... *Fern Weaver*

8 bacon strips
4 boneless skinless
    chicken breast halves
1 Tbsp. olive oil
½ tsp. salt
¼ tsp. pepper
2 small tomatoes, sliced
4 slices mozzarella cheese
6 fresh basil leaves, thinly sliced

Cook bacon, but not crispy. Set aside. Place chicken in an ungreased baking pan, brush with oil and sprinkle with salt and pepper. Top with tomatoes and basil, wrap each in 2 bacon strips, arranging bacon in a criss-cross on top of chicken. Bake uncovered at 350° for 35 minutes or till chicken is tender. Top with cheese and bake 1 minute longer. Yield: 4 servings.

Chicken Breasts over Pasta .... *Gina Mast*

2 raw chicken breasts, cut up
    in bite-size pieces
8 oz. cream cheese
Italian seasoning mix
1 can cream of mushroom soup
mushrooms, fresh or
    canned (optional)
pasta, cooked

Put all ingredients except pasta in crockpot on high for 4 hours. Cook your favorite pasta, serve chicken over pasta.

Chicken Bundles .... Lori Miller

Filling:
3 c. cooked chicken, cut up fine
⅔ c. mashed potatoes
¼ c. celery
¼ c. chicken broth
1 Tbsp. minced onions
1 Tbsp. parsley
½ tsp. salt

Crust:
2 c. flour
2 tsp. baking powder
½ tsp. salt
⅔ c. butter
½ c. milk

Filling: Mix filling ingredients together.
Crust: Mix flour, baking powder and salt together. Cut in butter until mixed like pie dough. Add milk. Press together lightly. Work dough only enough to hold together. Roll dough about ¼" thick and cut into 9 squares. Put ½ cup filling on each square. Bring up corners to center and fasten edges on top of bundle. Bake at 350° for 30 minutes. Serve with gravy.

Yield: 9 servings.

Chicken Delicious .... Glenda Weaver

Chicken breast
white American cheese
1 can cream of chicken soup
½ c. sour cream
¼ c. milk
1 box Stove Top chicken
1 box Stove Top corn bread
1 c. butter, melted

Layer 1: Layer chicken breast in bottom of 9"x13" pan. Cover chicken with white American cheese.
Layer 2: Mix together chicken soup, sour cream and milk. Pour over cheese slices.
Layer 3: Mix box of Stove Top chicken, Stove Top corn bread and butter together. Pour over soup. Cover and bake at 350° for 1 hour.

Yield: 8 servings.

Chicken Enchiladas .... *Lori Miller*

2 c. chicken, cooked and chopped
8 oz. cream cheese
1½ c. salsa or to taste
8 (6") flour tortillas
¾ lb. Velveeta cheese
¼ c. milk

Stir together chicken, cream cheese, and ½ cup salsa in sauce pan until cream cheese is melted. Spoon ⅓ cup chicken mixture on each tortilla and roll up. Heat milk and cheese till melted. Pour over top of tortillas. Cover and bake at 350° for 20 minutes. Serve with remaining salsa. You can also omit cheese sauce and serve with lettuce and tomatoes.
Yield: 8 servings.

Chicken Enchiladas .... *Esther Stoltzfus*

2 Tbsp. butter, softened
3 oz. cream cheese, softened
2 c. cooked chicken, diced
1 Tbsp. milk
½ tsp. salt
¼ tsp. cumin
1 can cream of chicken soup
1 c. sour cream
1 c. milk
⅓ c. jalapeño peppers
flour tortillas
shredded cheese

Mix butter, cream cheese, milk, salt, cumin, and chicken. Put ⅓ cup on a tortilla. Roll up and place seam side down in a baking dish. Mix together cream of chicken, sour cream, milk and peppers. Pour over tortillas and bake at 350° for 30 minutes or till heated through. Sprinkle with cheese and serve.

Chicken Enchiladas
.... Glenda Weaver

10 (7") flour tortillas
½ c. shredded cheddar cheese

Filling:
2½ c. cooked chicken
½ c. sour cream
1½ tsp. taco seasoning
½ can cream of
    mushroom soup
1 c. shredded cheddar cheese
1 small onion, chopped
½ c. salsa
¼ c. sliced olives

Sauce:
1 c. sour cream
1½ tsp. taco seasoning
½ can cream of mushroom soup

Filling: In bowl combine chopped chicken, sour cream, taco seasoning, soup, cheese, onions, salsa, and olives. Place ⅓ cup filling in each tortilla. Roll up and place seam side down in a greased 9"x13" pan.

Sauce: Combine remaining sour cream, taco seasoning, and soup. Pour over tortillas. Cover and bake at 350° for 30 minutes or until heated through. Sprinkle with cheese and return to oven until melted.

Yield: 8 servings.

Creamy Chicken Enchiladas
. Susanna Kanagy

4 oz. cream cheese, softened
1 Tbsp. water
1 tsp. onion powder
1 tsp. cumin
¼ tsp. salt
⅛ tsp. pepper
2½ c. chicken, cooked
    and chopped
10 (6") flour tortillas
1 can cream of chicken soup
1 c. sour cream
½ c. milk
1 (4 oz.) can green chilies
1 c. shredded cheddar cheese

In a bowl combine cream cheese, water, onion powder, cumin, salt and pepper. Stir in chicken. Divide evenly among tortillas. Roll up and place in a 9"x13" baking dish. Combine soup, sour cream, milk and green chilies. Pour over enchiladas. Bake at 350° for 30–40 minutes. Sprinkle with cheese and bake 5 more minutes.

Yield: 5-6 servings.

Chicken Noodles . . . . *Lill Stoltzfus*

1 c. butter
10 qt. chicken broth
3 Tbsp. salt
1 Tbsp. pepper
½ c. chicken base
4 lb. noodles
1 carrot, cooked and shredded
40 pieces cooked and deboned chicken

Brown butter in a 12 quart kettle. Add broth, salt, pepper and chicken base. Bring to a boil. Add noodles, and stir well. Turn off burner and let set 1 hour. (No lid lifting, or stirring.) Add chicken and carrots.
Note: Makes a roaster ¾ full. Holds for 5 hours if used for weddings or funerals. Recipe received from Susie Miller.
Yield: 30-35 servings.

Egg Rolls . . . . *Lori Miller*

1 head cabbage, sliced long and fine
1 sm. onion, cut fine
2 c. celery, cut fine
½ c. soy sauce
2 tsp. sugar
salt and pepper to taste
2 Tbsp. cornstarch
2 lb. chicken, cooked and cut fine.
egg roll wrappers

Sauté vegetables until crisp and tender (not soft) with soy sauce and sugar. Stir in remaining ingredients. Cook another 2 minutes. Cool before wrapping in egg roll wrappers. Place 1 tablespoon filling on wrapper. Roll up across the corner. Make a paste with water and cornstarch and paste corner. Fry and eat with duck sauce.
Note: Sausage may be used in place of chicken.

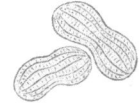

Four-Cheese Chicken Fettuccine . . Lori Miler

8 oz. fettuccine, cooked and drained
1 can cream of mushroom soup
4 oz. cream cheese, cubed
1 sm. can mushrooms, drained
1 c. milk
½ c. butter
¼ tsp. garlic powder
¾ c. grated Parmesan cheese
½ c. shredded mozzarella cheese
½ c. shredded Swiss cheese
2½ c. chicken, cooked and cubed
2 c. cooked vegetables (broccoli, carrots, cauliflower etc.)

In a large kettle combine soup, cream cheese, mushrooms, milk, butter and garlic powder. Stir in cheeses. Cook and stir until melted. Add chicken, heat through. Add fettuccine and vegetables to sauce.
Yield: 6-8 servings.

Chicken Spaghetti Casserole . . . . Fern Weaver

16 oz. angel-hair spaghetti
½ c. butter
32 oz. spaghetti sauce
peas (optional)
4 c. chicken, cooked
cheese

Cook spaghetti. Add butter, spaghetti sauce and peas. Stir in chicken, put in casserole dish, add cheese on top if you like. Bake at 350° for 20 minutes.
Yield: 12 servings.

Herb Chicken . . . . Valetta Yoder

½ c. soy sauce
½ c. lemon juice
4 cloves garlic, minced
1 tsp. cumin
1 tsp. basil
1 tsp. oregano
1 tsp. Italian seasoning
1 tsp. rosemary
6–8 chicken quarters

Marinate for a few hours. Grill chicken or make in a crockpot.

Japanese Chicken .... *Rachel Kanagy*

3 c. bite-size chicken breast pieces
flour
½ tsp. garlic powder
½ tsp. seasoned salt
½ tsp. paprika
2 Tbsp. flour

Sauce:

1 c. sugar
½ c. vinegar
3 Tbsp. soy sauce
½ c. water

Toss raw chicken pieces in flour and fry in hot oil about 3-4 minutes. Put chicken into 1½ quart casserole dish. Mix next four ingredients and toss with the chicken pieces. Mix the sauce ingredients together and pour over chicken. Bake uncovered at 350° for 45 minutes. Serve over white rice.

Yield: 4 servings.

Every outstanding success is built on the ability to do better than good enough.

Sesame Chicken .... Susan Miller

3 whole, boneless
   chicken breasts

Marinade:

2 Tbsp. flour
2 Tbsp. cornstarch
¼ tsp. baking powder
¼ tsp. baking soda
2 Tbsp. soy sauce
2 Tbsp. water
1 tsp. vegetable oil
olive oil (a few drops)

Sauce:

1 c. sugar, scant
¼ c. cornstarch
1 tsp. chili powder
½ c. water
2 Tbsp. vinegar
2 Tbsp. vegetable oil
1 clove garlic, minced
1 c. chicken broth
2 Tbsp. soy sauce
2 Tbsp. toasted sesame seeds

Cut chicken in bite-size pieces. Mix dry ingredients for marinade, then add oil, water and soy sauce. Marinate chicken several hours or overnight. Sauté chicken in small amount of oil or butter.

Sauce: Combine dry ingredients, then mix in remaining ingredients except sesame seeds. (Those can be toasted in a skillet without oil.) Cook and stir until sauce is clear and slightly thickened. Add sesame seeds. Combine chicken and sauce and serve with rice, or serve sauce on the side.

Yield: approximately 6-8 servings.

Spicy Chicken Casserole

Glenda Weaver and Amy Swartzentruber

16 oz. rotini pasta twists
4 c. chicken breast
½ c. chopped onions
1 c. butter
1 can cream of mushroom soup
1 can Rotel tomatoes with green chilies
1–2 lb. Velveeta cheese
½ tsp. garlic salt
½ tsp. poultry seasoning
¼ tsp. pepper

Cook pasta 8 minutes with enough chicken seasoning to make the water yellow. Drain, keeping 2 cups water. Fry onion and chicken in butter. Mix all ingredients plus the 2 cups water. Put in large casserole dish and bake at 350° for 35–40 minutes.

Note: Amy uses 1–1½ cups of the pasta water, and saves half of the cheese to sprinkle on top.

Yield: 8-10 servings.

Sour Cream Chicken

Renae Weaver

4 oz. chipped dried beef or thinly sliced ham
12 boneless, skinless chicken breasts
12 slices bacon, fried and crumbled
2 cans cream of mushroom soup
2 c. sour cream

Put chipped beef or ham in the bottom of a greased 9"x13" pan. Place chicken breasts on top. Sprinkle with crumbled bacon. Combine soup and sour cream and spread over top. Bake covered at 275° for 2 hours.

Yield: 8-10 servings.

Sweet and Sour Chicken ....*Susan Miller*

¼ c. butter
½ c. chopped onions
½ c. chopped green peppers
3 lb. chicken, cut up
¾ c. ketchup
¼ c. brown sugar
¾–1 c. pineapple juice
2 Tbsp. vinegar
2 tsp. soy sauce
½ tsp. garlic salt
½ tsp. salt
¼ tsp. pepper
1 (15 oz.) can chunk pineapple, drained

Sauté onions, peppers, and chicken in butter. Combine remaining ingredients except pineapple, Add to chicken mixture. Stir constantly till mixture boils. Add pineapple chunks. Simmer. Serve over rice.

Note: Optional—Add ¼–½ cup honey to increase sweetness.

Yield: 10-12 servings.

Sweet and Sour Chicken ....*Valetta Yoder*

1 pepper, chopped
1 onion, chopped
2 carrots, chopped
2 c. chicken breasts, chunked
1 (20 oz.) can pineapple
3 Tbsp. white vinegar
2 Tbsp. soy sauce
2 Tbsp. ketchup
⅓ c. brown sugar
2 Tbsp. cornstarch

Stir fry peppers, onions, carrots, and chicken in oil. Drain pineapple, save juice. Add enough water to make 1⅓ cups. Stir in vinegar, soy sauce, ketchup, brown sugar, and cornstarch. Gradually add to skillet. Bring to a boil and thicken. Reduce heat and simmer for several minutes. Add pineapple just before serving.

Baked Spaghetti .... *Alta Miller*

6 oz. thin spaghetti, dry
1 lb. ground beef
⅓ c. chopped onions
salt
pepper
45 oz. spaghetti sauce
2–3 c. shredded mozzarella cheese

Cook and drain spaghetti. Place in bottom of 9"x13" pan. Fry beef with chopped onions, salt and pepper. Sprinkle over spaghetti; then top with spaghetti sauce. Place shredded cheese on top. Bake at 350° until bubbly and cheese is slightly browned. Let set 5–10 minutes before serving.
Note: This can be made without the meat if desired.
Yield: 10-12 servings.

Yummy Spaghetti .... *Fern Weaver*

2½ lb. hamburger
1 (16 oz.) box thin spaghetti
1 can cream of mushroom soup
½ onion, chopped
½ tsp. salt
½ tsp. pepper
32 oz. spaghetti sauce
sour cream
shredded cheese

Brown hamburger with onion. Cook spaghetti and mix all together. Put in 9"x13" pan. Put sour cream and shredded cheese on top. Bake 20 minutes at 350° or until cheese is melted.
Yield: 10 servings.

Barbecued Meatballs .... *Tammy Yoder*

Meatballs:

1½ lb. ground beef
⅓ c. milk
½ c. oatmeal
½ c. Ritz cracker crumbs
1 egg
¼ c. chopped onions
¼ tsp. garlic powder
1 tsp. salt
¼ tsp. black pepper
1 tsp. chili powder

Sauce:

2 c. ketchup
½ c. brown sugar
½ tsp. liquid smoke flavoring
½ tsp. garlic powder
¼ c. onion chopped

Mix meatball ingredients together. Shape into balls. In a 9"x13" pan, layer meatballs single layer. In a separate bowl mix together sauce ingredients. Pour over meatballs. Bake, covered, at 325° for 2 hours.

Yield: 6-8 servings.

Barbecued Meatballs .... *Fannie Mae Kanagy*

3 lb. ground beef
1 (12 oz.) can evaporated milk
1 c. oatmeal
1 c. cracker crumbs
2 eggs
½ c. chopped onions
½ tsp. garlic powder
2 tsp. salt
½ tsp. pepper
2 tsp. chili powder

Sauce:

2 c. ketchup
1 c. brown sugar
½ tsp. liquid smoke or to taste
½ tsp. garlic powder
¼ c. chopped onions

To make meatballs, combine all ingredients, (mixture will be soft) and shape into walnut-size balls. Place meatballs in a single layer on wax paper-lined cookie sheets. Freeze until solid. Store frozen meatballs in freezer bags until ready to cook.

Sauce: Combine all ingredients. Stir until sugar is dissolved. Place frozen meatballs in a 9"x13" baking pan, pour on the sauce. Bake at 350° for 1 hour.

Yield: 80 meatballs.

Barbecued Spareribs .... *Fannie Mae Kanagy*

4 lb. pork spareribs cut into serving size pieces
1 c. barbecue sauce

Marinade Sauce:

1 c. soy sauce
½ c. vinegar
¼ c. brown sugar
¼ c. minced onions
2 Tbsp. vegetable oil
1 Tbsp. minced garlic
1 tsp. ground ginger
¼ tsp. pepper

Place spareribs in marinade container with tight fitting lid. Mix marinade sauce and pour over ribs. Marinate 6 hours or more. Place ribs on a hot grill and grill about 20 minutes. Brushing with barbecue sauce. Place in roast pan, brush again with barbecue sauce. Cover tightly and bake at 275° for 2 hours or until tender.

Enchilada Casserole .... *Tammy Yoder*

1 lb. ground beef
½ c. chopped onions
1 (16 oz.) can refried beans
2 tsp. chili powder
½ tsp. garlic powder
1 (15 oz.) can tomato sauce
2 cans cream of mushroom soup
½–¾ c. sour cream
¾ c. milk
10 flour tortillas
shredded cheese

In a skillet, fry beef and onions. Add refried beans, chili powder, garlic powder and tomato sauce. Divide meat mixture evenly among 10 tortilla shells, roll up. In a separate bowl, mix together cream of mushroom soup, sour cream and milk. In a 9"x13" pan, pour half of the soup mixture in pan, add tortillas and pour rest of soup mixture over tortillas. Top with shredded cheese. Bake at 350° for 30 minutes.

Garlic Beef Enchiladas

Elsie Yoder

1 lb. ground beef
1 med. onion, chopped
2 Tbsp. flour
1 Tbsp. chili powder
1 tsp. salt
1 tsp. garlic powder
½ tsp. ground cumin
1 (14.5 oz.) can stewed tomatoes

Sauce:

4–6 cloves garlic, minced
⅓ c. butter
½ c. flour
1 (14.5 oz.) can beef broth
1 (15 oz.) can tomato sauce
1 Tbsp. chili powder
1 tsp. ground cumin
½ tsp. salt
10 (7") flour tortillas
2 c. Colby Monterey Jack cheese, shredded

Cook beef and onion until meat is no longer pink. Drain and add flour and seasonings, mix well. Stir in tomatoes; bring to a boil. Reduce heat; cover and simmer for 15 minutes.

Sauce: In a saucepan, sauté garlic in butter until tender. Stir in flour until blended. Gradually stir in broth, bring to a boil. Cook and stir 2 minutes or until bubbly. Stir in tomato sauce and seasonings, heat through. Pour about 1¼ cup sauce in ungreased 9"x13" baking dish. Spread about ¼ cup beef mixture down the center of each tortilla, top with 2 tablespoons cheese, Roll up tightly, place seam side down over sauce. Top with remaining sauce. Cover, bake at 350° for 30–35 minutes. Sprinkle with remaining cheese. Bake uncovered 10–15 minutes longer or until cheese is melted.

Yield: 4-6 servings.

Fried Empanadas.....................Valetta Yoder

Dough:
3 c. flour
1½ tsp. baking powder
6 Tbsp. Crisco
1 c. milk

Filling:
1 lb. hamburger
1 onion, chopped
1 pepper, chopped
onion salt
pepper
garlic salt
cumin
chili powder
6 hard-boiled eggs

Mix dough ingredients as pie dough. Roll dough out thinly into 4" circles. Fill with filling.
Filling: Sauté hamburger, onion, and pepper until brown. Add seasonings to taste. Fry. Last add hard-boiled eggs and mix. Place a spoonful of meat mixture into each shell. Fold edge of pastry shell over and press edges together. Wet edge of dough before pinching shut. Fry in hot oil until golden brown. Other options for filling are chicken or ham and cheese.
Note: Keep dough moist when mixing. Add more flour as needed when rolling out.
Yield: 20 Empanadas.

Burrito Casserole....................Ruth Weaver

1 lb. ground beef
1 (15 oz.) can refried beans
1 env. taco seasoning
8 sm. flour tortillas
2 c. sour cream
1 can cream of
   mushroom soup
shredded cheddar cheese
tomatoes, chopped
lettuce, chopped
salsa
additional sour cream

Fry ground beef. Add beans and taco seasoning. Spread 1 heaping tablespoon on each tortilla and roll up. Mix sour cream and cream of mushroom soup. Spread some on bottom of a 9"x13" baking pan. Lay burritos on top. Spread remaining soup mixture on top of burritos. Bake at 350° for 30 minutes, add shredded cheese on top and return to oven long enough for cheese to melt. Serve with tomatoes, lettuce, salsa and sour cream.
Yield: 8 servings.

Deep Dish Taco Squares .... *Renae Weaver*

2 c. Bisquick baking mix
½ c. cold water
1 lb. ground beef, browned
1½ Tbsp. taco seasoning
¾ c. pizza sauce
1 c. sour cream
½ c. mayonnaise
1½ c. shredded cheddar cheese
2 Tbsp. minced onions

Combining Bisquick and water; press into a greased 9"x13" pan. Combine ground beef, taco seasoning, and pizza sauce; spread over crust. Combine remaining ingredients and spread over meat mixture. Bake uncovered at 350° for 25–30 minutes.
Yield: 12 servings.

Mexican Dish .... *Lori Miller*

1 lb. hamburger
¼ c. chopped onions or to taste
1 c. refried beans
1 pkg. taco seasoning
¾ c. salsa
1 tube crescent rolls
1 c. sour cream
2 c. cheese
1 c. chips
lettuce
tomatoes, chopped

Fry hamburger and onions, then add taco seasoning, refried beans and salsa. Place crescents rolls in a 9"x13" pan and top with meat mixture. Bake at 350° for 20 minutes. Add sour cream, cheese, and chips. Bake 10 minutes. Serve with lettuce and tomatoes.

Mexican Lasagna...............Susan Miller

1½ lb. ground beef
½ tsp. cumin
1 Tbsp. chili powder
¼ tsp. garlic powder
¼ tsp. red pepper
1 tsp. salt
1 tsp. pepper
16 oz. salsa
10–12 flour tortillas
cheese sauce
2 c. shredded cheese
½ c. diced tomatoes
3 green onions, chopped
½ c. shredded cheese,

Brown ground beef and add next seven ingredients. Cut tortillas into bite size pieces and put half in bottom of 9"x13" pan. Put half of meat mixture on top, then half of cheese sauce. (Use cheese sauce of your choice or use shredded cheese.) Repeat layers. Bake until heated through. Just before serving, top with lettuce, tomatoes, onions and cheese. Serve with sour cream if desired.
Yield: approximately 8-10 servings.

Pizza Rice..........................Rachel Kanagy

1 lb. ground beef
½ tsp. salt
¼ tsp. pepper
4 c. cooked rice
2 c. pizza sauce
2 c. shredded mozzarella cheese
pepperoni slices

Brown ground beef and season with salt and pepper. In a casserole dish, layer ½ of rice, ground beef, pizza sauce, cheese, then pepperoni. Make second layer with other half of ingredients. Bake 30–40 minutes at 350° until heated through and cheese is melted.
Yield: 10 servings.

Tortilla Stacks .... *Elsie Yoder*

½ lb. ground beef or turkey
2 cloves garlic, minced
1 c. Ortega thick and
    chunky salsa, divided
1 (16 oz.) can refried beans
½ c. green onions, thinly sliced
12 (7") flour or corn tortillas
2 c. 4 cheese
    Mexican Blend, divided
sour cream
fresh cilantro, chopped,
    (optional)

Brown ground beef with garlic, stir in ½ cup salsa, beans and green onions. Cook 5 minutes. Place tortillas on foil-lined baking sheet. Spread half of bean mixture evenly over tortillas, spreading to edges. Use about ⅓ cup bean mixture for each tortilla. Top with ¾ cup cheese. Repeat layering with four more tortillas, remaining bean mixture and ¾ cup cheese, spoon remaining ½ cup salsa evenly over tortillas spreading to edges. Bake at 350° for 10 minutes. Sprinkle with remaining ½ cup cheese. Bake 5 minutes or until heated. Garnish with sour cream and cilantro.
Yield: 4-6 servings.

Vietnam Fried Rice .... *Renae Weaver*

3 c. cooked rice
¼ c. vegetable oil
¼–½ lb. any cooked
    or raw meat
garlic and onions to taste
1 tsp. salt
1 tsp. sugar
1 tsp. pepper
1 Tbsp. soy sauce
2 eggs

Heat oil in skillet and sauté all ingredients except eggs. When ready to serve, scramble the eggs into rice mixture until cooked.
Note: An easy and good way to use leftover rice.
Yield: 2 servings.

Glorified Texas Hash .... *Rachel Kanagy*

2 lb. hamburger
4 c. tomato juice
1 c. uncooked rice
1 Tbsp. taco seasoning
1 Tbsp. chili powder
⅓ c. sugar
2 Tbsp. vinegar
2 tsp. salt

Toppings:

1 c. sour cream
1 c. salad dressing
1½ c. shredded cheddar cheese

Brown hamburger. Mix all other ingredients together and add to hamburger. Pour in 2 quart casserole dish. Bake uncovered at 350° for 50 minutes or until rice is tender. Mix sour cream and salad dressing together. Spread over top of rice. Sprinkle cheese over cream. Bake a few more minutes until cheese is melted.
Note: This is an easy and delicious all-in-one dish.
Yield: 6-8 servings.

Popover Pizza .... *Fannie Mae Kanagy*

1 lb. ground beef
1 env. spaghetti sauce mix
1¾ c. water
6 oz. tomato paste
8 oz. mozzarella cheese, shredded
2 eggs
1 c. milk
1 Tbsp. vegetable oil
1 c. flour
½ tsp. salt
Parmesan cheese

In a medium saucepan, brown ground beef; pour off excess fat. Add the spaghetti sauce mix, water, and tomato paste; simmer 10 minutes, stirring occasionally. Spoon into greased 9"x13" pan. Top with mozzarella cheese. Keep hot in 400° oven. Beat together until smooth, the eggs, milk, oil, flour and salt; pour over filling. Sprinkle with Parmesan cheese. Bake at 400° for 30 minutes.
Yield: 6-8 servings.

Zucchini Pizza Casserole

Elsie Yoder and Valetta Yoder

4 c. unpeeled zucchini, shredded
½ tsp. salt
2 eggs
½ c. grated Parmesan cheese,
1 c. grated cheddar cheese, divided,
2 c. grated mozzarella cheese, divided
1 lb. ground beef
½ c. chopped onions
1 (15 oz.) can Italian flavor tomato sauce
¼ tsp. oregano
¼ tsp. basil
1 med. green pepper, chopped

Place zucchini in strainer. Sprinkle with salt, and let drain for 10 minutes. Squeeze out moisture and combine zucchini with eggs, Parmesan cheese and half of the cheddar and mozzarella cheese. Press into greased 9"x13" baking pan. Bake at 400° for 20 minutes. Meanwhile brown ground beef with onions. Drain and add the tomato sauce, oregano and basil. Spoon over baked zucchini mixture. Top with remaining cheeses and sprinkle with chopped green peppers. Bake for 20 minutes more.
Yield: 6-8 servings.

Mini Cheddar Loaves

Alta Miller

1 egg
¾ c. milk
1 c. shredded cheddar cheese,
½ c. oatmeal
½ c. chopped onions
1 tsp. salt
1 lb. ground beef

Sauce:
⅔ c. ketchup
½ c. brown sugar
1½ tsp. mustard

Mix all ingredients. Shape into 8 loaves. Place on baking sheet.
Sauce: Mix ingredients and spread or drizzle over loaves. Bake at 350° for 45 minutes.
Yield: 8 servings.

Potato Haystack Casserole..... *Glenda Weaver*

2½ lb. potatoes
1 pkg. ranch dressing mix
1 c. sour cream
¾ c. milk
2 lb. hamburger
1 onion, chopped
1 pkg. taco seasoning
salt and pepper to taste
corn chips

Cheese Sauce:

¼ c. butter
¼ c. flour
½ tsp. salt
2 c. milk
2½ c. Velveeta cheese

Cook, peel, and grate potatoes. Mix in ranch, sour cream and milk. Put in bottom of 9"x13" pan. Brown and drain hamburger and chopped onions. Add taco seasoning, salt and pepper to taste. Layer hamburger on top of potatoes. Top with cheese sauce. Bake at 350° for 40 minutes. Just before eating, top with crumbled corn chips.

Cheese Sauce: Melt butter, add flour and salt. Cook until smooth, then stir in milk and bring to a boil. Add cheese and stir until melted.

Yield: 10 servings.

Black Eyed Peas with Ham..... *Susanna Kanagy*

1 med. onion, chopped
2 T. vegetable oil
1 c. cooked ham, chopped
1 clove garlic, minced
2 (15 oz.) cans black eyed peas, drained
1 (14 oz.) can chicken broth
1 tsp. rubbed sage
½ tsp. dried thyme
½ tsp. pepper
hot cooked rice

Toppings:

chopped tomatos
sliced green onions
hot pepper sauce

In medium saucepan, sauté onions in oil for 3 minutes. Stir in ham and garlic, sauté 3 minutes. Add peas, broth and seasonings. Simmer 20 minutes. Serve over rice with desired toppings.

Yield: 6 servings.

Scalloped Potatoes with Ham - large recipe .... *Fern Weaver*

8 bags hash browns or 20 lb. potatoes, cooked and shredded
5 lb. ham, cubed
3 qt. heavy cream
2 lb. Velveeta cheese
salt and pepper to taste

Layer potatoes, ham, and cheese in a big electric roaster. Put a little salt and pepper on each layer. Pour cream over all. Bake at 250° for 3 hours. Do not stir until ready to serve.
Yield: 40 servings.

Scalloped Potatoes with Ham .... *Ruth Weaver*

2½ lb. potatoes
½ c. butter
2 cans cream of chicken soup
8 oz. Velveeta cheese
1½ c. sour cream
salt and pepper to taste
1½ lb. cooked ham
2 Tbsp. melted butter
2 c. cornflake crumbs

Wash, peel, and cook potatoes. Cool, then shred or slice. Melt ½ cup butter in a medium saucepan. Add soup, cheese, sour cream, salt and pepper. Heat until cheese is melted, stirring constantly. Pour over potatoes, cut ham in ½" cubes and stir into potatoes. Mix well then place in a large greased casserole dish. Combine melted butter and cornflake crumbs. Put on top and bake covered for 45 minutes at 350°. Uncover and bake another 10 minutes or until heated through.
Yield: 10-12 servings.

Smoked Sausage Skillet .... *Elsie Yoder*

1 lb. fully cooked kielbasa or Polish sausage, sliced
3 c. shredded cabbage
1 celery rib, finely chopped
1 Tbsp. vegetable oil
2 Tbsp. Dijon mustard
½ tsp. garlic salt
¼ tsp. rubbed sage
2 c. cooked noodles

In a large skillet, sauté the sausage, cabbage and celery in oil for 5 minutes. Add the mustard, garlic salt and sage. Cook and stir over medium heat for 4–6 minutes or until vegetables are tender. Stir in noodles and heat through.

Yield: 4 servings.

Pork Roast .... *Susanna Kanagy*

4–5 lb. pork roast
½ tsp. salt
¼ tsp. pepper
1 clove garlic, slivered
2 onions, sliced
2 bay leaves
1 whole clove
1 c. hot water
2 Tbsp. soy sauce

Rub roast with salt and pepper. Using a sharp knife, cut slits in roast and fill with garlic slivers. Place on baking sheet and broil until browned. In a roaster or crockpot, put one sliced onion. Lay roast on top of onions and layer with remaining onion. Combine bay leaves, clove, water and soy sauce. Pour over roast. Cover tightly with foil. Bake at 300° for 2½ hours, then at 275° for 3 hours or until roast is very tender. Crockpot option: Low for 10 hours or high for 5–6 hours.

Yield: 8-12 servings.

Scrumptious Beef .... *Alta Miller*

2 lb. stew beef
8 oz. mushrooms
2 c. beef broth
2 med. onions, chopped
1 can cream of celery soup
1 pkg. onion gravy mix

Place raw meat in a large casserole dish or medium roaster. Add remaining ingredients. No need to mix. Bake uncovered at 300° for 6 hours. Serve with noodles, rice, potatoes or biscuits. No salt or additional seasoning needed.
Yield: 8-12 servings.

Wrapped Venison Steak .... *LaVerda Weaver*

Venison cube steaks
bacon
1 pkg. onion soup mix
Dale's seasoning sauce
fresh mushrooms
   whole or halved
onions

Wrap each steak with bacon and put in casserole dish, or roaster pan. Sprinkle with soup mix and Dale's seasoning sauce. Put mushrooms and onions over top. If you have more than goes into a 9"x13" pan you need more soup mix, and seasonings. Bake at 350° for 1 hour.

Beaufort Stew .... *Gina Mast*

9–10 lb. shrimp
15–20 sm. ears corn
2 (3 oz.) bags crab boil
   seasoning
3 rings sausage, chunked to
   serving size

This works best outdoors in a big pot with a strainer. Bring water to boiling with crab boil bags, put in corn. Bring back to a boil, then add sausage. Bring back to a boil, and add shrimp. Bring back to boil for 3 minutes.
Yield: 10 servings.

Grilled Honey Bacon Fish ..... *Susanna Kanagy*

16 bacon strips, partially cooked
8 fish fillets (such as Tilapia)
1 c. thinly sliced onions
¼ c. butter, melted
2 Tbsp. honey
½ tsp. salt
¼ tsp. pepper

Using shallow foil pans or heavy duty tinfoil sheets (with sides folded up) layer bacon, (using two strips per fish fillet) fish and onion. Drizzle with butter and honey. Sprinkle with salt and pepper. Cover pans with additional foil and grill over medium heat 12–15 minutes or until fish flakes with fork.
Yield: 8 servings.

Fettuccine Alfredo .... *Renae Weaver*

½ c. butter
8 oz. cream cheese
2 tsp. garlic powder
2 c. milk
¾ c. Parmesan cheese
dash of salt and pepper
½ lb. fettuccine

Melt butter. Add cream cheese and garlic powder, stirring with a whisk until smooth. Add milk, a little at a time, whisking to smooth out lumps. Stir in Parmesan, salt and pepper. Remove from heat when sauce reaches desired consistency. Cook fettuccine according to directions on package. Combine noodles and sauce and serve immediately.
Note: Optional—stir in grilled chicken breasts or cooked shrimp for a one dish meal.
Yield: 4-6 servings.

Lime Honey Glazed Salmon ... *LaVerda Weaver*

6 salmon fillets

Glaze:
¼ c. extra virgin olive oil
1 med. red onion, chopped
½ tsp. red pepper
1 tsp. cumin
1 tsp. pepper
juice of 3 lemons or limes
3 Tbsp. honey or agave
1 tsp. chili powder
1 red bell pepper, chopped
2 lg. cloves garlic, minced

Black Bean and Corn Salsa:
1 can corn, drained or 10 oz. frozen corn
1 c. black beans, drained
½ c. chicken broth
6 c. baby spinach
fresh cilantro

Glaze: Chop and mix all ingredients and put over salmon fillets. (Best when put on at least a few hours before grilling.) Grill and serve with black bean salsa.

Salsa: Make another glaze recipe and add remaining salsa ingredients.

Shrimp and Grits ... *Lill Stoltzfus*

2½ c. chicken broth or water
¼ c. butter, divided
¾ c. grits
3 Tbsp. cream cheese
2 Tbsp. half and half
1 lb. medium shrimp, peeled and deveined
2 Tbsp. fresh lime juice
salt and pepper
cheese
¾ c. cheddar cheese, (optional)
½ c. chopped green onions

Combine broth and 1 tablespoon butter in heavy saucepan. Bring to a boil. Stir in grits. Reduce heat. Cover and simmer approximately 7 more minutes, stirring occasionally. Add cream cheese and half and half. Melt remaining butter in large heavy skillet. Sauté shrimp about 3 minutes, just until pink. Stir in lime juice, salt, pepper, and cheese. Spoon grits on plate. Top with shrimp and sprinkle green onions over all.

Yield: 3 servings.

Shrimp and Grits . . . . *Fern Weaver*

Grits:

3 c. water
1 c. milk
¼ c. butter
1 tsp. salt
1 c. quick cooking grits
cheese (optional)

Shrimp:

1 lb. raw shrimp peeled
½ c. butter
2 Tbsp. lemon juice
1 tsp. Worcestershire sauce
1 tsp. soy sauce
1 tsp. parsley flakes
¼ tsp. salt
⅛ tsp. pepper
⅛ tsp. garlic powder

Grits: Bring milk and water to a boil, add salt, butter and grits. Cook 5 minutes. Whisk to make grits nice and smooth.

Shrimp: Put all seasonings and butter in saucepan. Bring to boiling, then add shrimp and cook until shrimp are pink, approximately 3 minutes. Pour shrimp and seasonings into grits and mix it all together. You can also serve with cheese on top.

Yield: 4-5 servings.

Shrimp and Rice Casserole . . . . *LaVerda Weaver*

3 c. cooked rice
2 Tbsp. chopped green peppers
2 Tbsp. chopped onions
2 Tbsp. butter, melted
2 Tbsp. lemon juice
½ tsp. dry mustard
¼ tsp. black pepper
1 can cream of mushroom soup
½ c. cheese, cubed or shredded

Mix all ingredients thoroughly. Pour into greased casserole dish and bake uncovered at 375° for 30–35 minutes.

Note: Regular mustard is okay too.

Yield: 4 servings.

Shrimp Scampi........................ *Elsie Yoder*

1–1½ lb. shrimp
¾ c. butter
2–3 cloves garlic minced
½ c. sliced green onions
1 Tbsp. fresh lemon juice
1 Tbsp. Worcestershire sauce
⅛ tsp. cayenne pepper
1 Tbsp. fresh parsley, minced
¼ c. dry white wine

Peel and devein shrimp, but leave tail attached. Melt butter in sauté pan, add garlic and onions and sauté over low heat until golden. Add remaining ingredients, and allow to bubble for 1 minute then remove from heat. Pour shrimp on ovenproof platter. Pour half the garlic butter over shrimp and broil five inches from heat for 3 minutes. Turn shrimp over and top with remaining butter mixture and broil an additional 3 minutes. Yield: 4 servings.

Stir Fry.................................. *Lill Stoltzfus*

1½ c. brown rice
butter or bacon grease
2 eggs
2 onions, chopped
8 oz. fresh mushrooms, sliced
1 red bell pepper, sliced
1 lg. carrot, sliced
1½ c. shredded cabbage
1 lb. raw shrimp
3 chicken breasts, cut in strips and marinated in pineapple juice or Italian dressing
¼ c. soy sauce (or to taste)
½ c. stir fry sauce (optional)
fresh parsley

Cook rice (leftover rice may also be used) according to package directions. Cool. In skillet, sauté rice in butter or bacon grease, stirring constantly. Add eggs and stir fry until done. In another skillet stir fry onions, mushrooms, peppers, carrot and cabbage. (I stir fry each one separately until crisp and tender.) Stir fry chicken in butter until cooked. Stir fry shrimp in butter until shrimp turn pink. Combine fried rice, vegetables, soy sauce, and stir fry sauce. (I use La Choy Stir Fry Original.)

Note: Top with chicken and shrimp. Garnish with fresh parsley.

Shrimp and Wild Rice Casserole

Amy Swartzentruber

1 can cream of mushroom soup
2 Tbsp. chopped green bell peppers
2 Tbsp. butter, melted
1 Tbsp. lemon juice
2 c. cooked rice (or more)
½ tsp. Worcestershire sauce
½ tsp. dry mustard
½ c. grated cheese
½ lb. shrimp, raw and cleaned

Mix all ingredients thoroughly. Pour into a greased 1½ qt. casserole dish. Bake at 375° for 30–35 minutes.

Yield: 4 servings.

Anna's Marinade

Lill Stoltzfus

1 c. soy sauce
¾ c. molasses
¼ c. lemon juice
¼ c. olive oil
2 Tbsp. fresh ginger, minced or 1 tsp. ginger
2 cloves garlic, minced
¾ tsp. pepper

Mix all ingredients and pour over pork tender-loin or chops for at least 24 hours, then grill. Enjoy!

Chicken Marinade

Glenda Weaver

Italian dressing
Dale's seasoning
water

Equal amounts of everything. Mix together and marinate chicken overnight.

Chicken Marinade .... *Rachel Kanagy*

⅔ c. vegetable oil
¼ c. vinegar
⅓ c. lemon juice
6 Tbsp. sugar
1 tsp. parsley
¼ tsp. garlic powder
¼ tsp. onion powder
1 tsp. salt

Mix all ingredients well. Pour over chicken and marinate overnight. Grill and enjoy!

Note: We like to cut chicken breasts into strips and use this marinade. We eat them with barbecue sauce, in fajitas, or grilled chicken salad!
Yield: 1½ cup marinade.

Chicken Barbecue Marinade ..... *Lill Stolztfus*

1 qt. apple cider vinegar
1 Tbsp. Worcestershire sauce
½ c. salt
1 c. butter
dash of pepper

In saucepan heat 2 cups of the vinegar, Worcestershire sauce, salt, butter and pepper. Stir until salt and butter are dissolved. Remove from heat. Add remaining vinegar. Pour over chicken and marinate for at least 24 hours. Grill.

Barbecue Sauce .... *Valetta Yoder*

1 c. ketchup
½ c. brown sugar
⅓ c. sugar
¼ c. honey
¼ c. molasses or Karo
2 tsp. mustard
1½ tsp. Worcestershire sauce
¼ tsp. salt
¼ tsp. liquid smoke
⅛ tsp. pepper

Mix together and heat until sugar is dissolved.

Grilled Ham Marinade .... Lill Stoltzfus

2 c. pineapple juice
1 tsp. vinegar
1 Tbsp. lemon juice
½ tsp. salt
1½ c. brown sugar
¾ tsp. dry mustard
1 (20 oz.) can ring pineapple
1 average size ham, sliced thick

Mix first 6 ingredients and pour over ham at least 24 hours. We usually do for 30 hours. Grill over charcoal just to brown a little. Also grill pineapple rings, to scatter over meat. We've done this for several weddings.

Yield: 5 servings.

Steak Marinade .... Valetta Yoder

1 c. lemon juice
1 c. vinegar
1 c. vegetable oil
1 c. soy sauce
1 c. tomato paste
½ c. asado salt–or ¼ c. salt
1 onion, chopped
6 cloves garlic, minced
10–15 steaks

Marinate a few hours or overnight. Grill.

When a jar cover sticks, run hot water over the lid for a minute. It should then open easily.

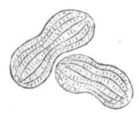

Vegetables and Sides

Recipe featured on previous page:
Southern Macaroni Pie *page 129*

Roasted Asparagus............ *Susanna Kanagy*

1 lb. asparagus, trimmed
olive oil
sea salt

Spread asparagus in single layer on baking sheet. Drizzle with olive oil and sprinkle with sea salt. Bake at 475° for 10 minutes.
Yield: 4 servings.

Baked Beans....................*Susan Miller*

5 slices bacon, chopped
½ c. chopped onions
4 (15 oz.) cans pork & beans
1½ c. brown sugar
3 Tbsp. ketchup
1 tsp. mustard
1 Tbsp. Worcestershire sauce
1 Tbsp. liquid smoke
dash of oregano
dash of salt and pepper
dash of parsley flakes

Fry bacon and chopped onions in skillet until bacon is crisp. Add remaining ingredients and mix well. Bake, uncovered, in 9"x13" baking dish for 2 hours at 350°.
Yield: 15-20 servings.

Mom's Baked Beans............... *Elsie Yoder*

1 lb. dry great northern beans
   or 4 cans northern
   beans, drained
1 lb. bacon
2 c. ketchup
1½ c. brown sugar
¾ c. pancake syrup

Soak dry beans overnight in cold water. In the morning, drain; and add 2 quarts fresh water. Cook till almost tender; drain off liquid. Fry and cut up bacon. Add bacon and drippings to beans. Add the rest of ingredients and bake at 350° for 1½ hours.
Yield: 8-10 servings.

Broccoli Casserole .... Fern Weaver

2 (10 oz.) pkg. frozen broccoli
1 can cream of mushroom soup
1 c. grated cheese
¾ c. mayonnaise
2 eggs, beaten
2 Tbsp. chopped onions
½ c. cracker crumbs

Cook broccoli for 5 minutes and drain, put in buttered casserole dish. Layer cream of mushroom soup, cheese, mayonnaise, eggs and onions. Sprinkle crackers on top. Bake 350° for 30 minutes.
Yield: 4-5 servings.

Broccoli Elegant .... Fannie Mae Kanagy

1½ c. water
5 Tbsp. butter, divided
1 (6 oz.) pkg. chicken flavor stuffing mix
2 (10 oz.) pkg. frozen broccoli spears, thawed and drained
2 tsp. all-purpose flour
1 tsp. chicken bouillon
¾ c. milk
3 oz. cream cheese, softened
¼ tsp. salt
1 med. onion, finely chopped
¾ c. shredded cheddar cheese
paprika

Preheat oven to 350°. Grease a 9"x13" baking dish. Combine water and 3 tablespoons butter in large saucepan. Bring to a boil. Remove from heat. Stir in stuffing and let set 5 minutes. Spoon stuffing around edge of baking dish, leaving a well in the center. Arrange broccoli spears in well. Melt remaining 2 tablespoons butter over medium low heat. Add flour, stirring till smooth. Cook 1 minute. Stir constantly. Add chicken bouillon and milk gradually; cook over medium heat until thickened, about 3 minutes. Stir constantly. Whisk in cream cheese and salt till smooth. Stir in onion. Pour sauce over broccoli. Sprinkle with cheddar cheese and paprika. Cover with foil and bake 35 minutes. Remove foil and bake 10 minutes longer.
Yield: 8 servings.

California Blend Casserole ..... *Glenda Weaver*

2 (16 oz.) bags California blend
1 can cream of mushroom soup
½ c. sour cream
½ lb. Velveeta cheese
salt
pepper

Cook California blend until soft. Mix everything and put in a 9"x13" pan. Top with combined crackers and butter. Bake at 350° for 45 minutes.
Yield: 8 servings.

Topping:
1 pkg. Ritz crackers, crushed
½ c. butter, melted

Colorful Veggies .... *Esther Stoltzfus*

2 (16 oz.) pkg. California Blend vegetables
8 oz. Velveeta cheese, cubed
6 Tbsp. butter, divided
½ c. crushed crackers

Cook vegetables, place half in an ungreased 7"x11" baking dish. In a small saucepan, combine cheese and 4 tablespoon butter, cook over low heat till melted. Pour half over veggies. Repeat layers. Melt remaining butter, and toss with cracker crumbs. Sprinkle over top. Bake uncovered at 325° for 20–25 minutes or until golden brown.
Yield: 8–10 servings.

Baked Corn Casserole............. Lori Miller

1 c. broccoli, fresh or frozen
1 pt. corn, fresh or frozen
salt
pepper
1⅓ c. crushed saltine crackers
1 c. milk
¼ lb. Velveeta cheese
1–2 Tbsp. butter

In a saucepan cook broccoli till tender; drain. Chop broccoli as desired. In a greased casserole dish, place broccoli, corn, salt, pepper and cracker crumbs. Mix together. Add milk and cheese. Dot with butter. Bake uncovered at 350° for 45 minutes or until set.
Note: More cheese and milk can be added.
Yield: 4-6 servings.

Scalloped Corn................... Katie Stoltzfus

2 eggs
1 c. milk
⅔ c. cracker or bread crumbs
2 c. canned or frozen corn
1 tsp. minced onion
½ tsp. salt
⅛ tsp. pepper
1 Tbsp. sugar
3 Tbsp. butter, melted

Beat the eggs, add milk and crumbs. Add the corn, onion, seasonings, and melted butter. Mix together well and pour in a greased casserole dish. Bake at 350° for 40 minutes.
Yield: 6 servings.

BBQ Green Beans............. Susanna Kanagy

10 slices bacon, chopped
¼ c. chopped onions
¾ c. ketchup
¼ c. brown sugar
1 Tbsp. Worcestershire sauce
¾ tsp. salt
4 c. green beans, cooked or
   1 qt. canned green beans, drained

Fry bacon until crisp. Remove from pan and add onion to drippings. Sauté until tender. Add ketchup, brown sugar, Worcestershire sauce and salt to onions. Put green beans in a 2 qt. baking dish. Pour sauce over beans and top with bacon. Bake at 300° for 35–40 minutes or until bubbly.
Serves 4–6 people.

Hush Puppies........................ *Renae Weaver*

2 eggs, beaten
½ c. sugar
1 lg. onion, chopped
¾ c. self-rising flour
1 c. self-rising cornmeal
1 qt. oil for frying

In a medium bowl, mix together eggs, sugar and onion. Blend in flour and cornmeal. Heat 2 inches of oil to 365°. Drop batter by rounded teaspoonfuls in hot oil, and fry until golden brown. Cook in small batches to maintain oil temperature. Drain briefly on paper towels.
Yield: 8 servings.

Onion Rings........................... *Lori Miller*

Breading:

onions
milk
eggs
¾ c. flour
½ c. cornmeal (scant)
seasoning salt
pepper
salt
paprika

Dip onion rings in milk and egg. Mix breading ingredients together. Roll in breading mixture. Can repeat breadings if desired. Fry and enjoy.

Note: These taste like Sonic onion rings.

Baked Lemon Pasta .... *Susan Miller*

1 lb. thin spaghetti
¼ c. butter
2 Tbsp. olive oil
2 cloves garlic, minced
juice of one lemon
zest of one lemon
2 c. sour cream
½ tsp. salt
Parmesan cheese, grated
flat leaf parsley (optional)
additional lemon juice

Cook spaghetti according to package directions. In skillet, melt butter with olive oil over low heat. Add garlic. Squeeze lemon juice into skillet and turn off heat. Add sour cream and stir. Add lemon zest and salt. Pour over drained spaghetti and stir. Bake covered at 375° for 15 minutes, then uncover and bake for 7–10 more minutes. Remove from oven and squeeze additional lemon juice over top. Then top generously with Parmesan cheese and chopped parsley. Add final squeeze of lemon juice just before serving if desired.
Note: Goes very well with grilled chicken.
Yield: 8-10 servings.

Baked Macaroni and Cheese .. *Rachel Kanagy*

2 c. elbow macaroni
4 c. water
1 tsp. salt
¼ c. butter
3 Tbsp. flour
2 c. milk
2 c. shredded cheddar cheese
¾ tsp. salt
¾ tsp. mustard
¼ tsp. pepper

Cook macaroni in water and salt for 8 minutes. Drain. In a separate saucepan, melt butter. Stir in flour until bubbly. Stir in milk and bring to a boil. Stir cheese, salt, mustard, and pepper into sauce. Mix pasta and sauce in a large bowl and pour into a 9"x13" pan. Bake at 350° for 35 minutes or until golden and sides are bubbly.
Yield: 10 servings.

Southern Macaroni Pie .... *Susan Miller*

¾ c. macaroni
1½ c. milk
3 eggs, beaten
2 Tbsp. butter
½ lb. grated cheddar cheese
salt to taste

Boil macaroni in salted water. Drain. Add milk, eggs, butter and cheese. Add salt to taste. Bake at 350° until not quite set.
Yield: 6 servings.

Fried Mushrooms .... *Glenda Weaver*

¼ c. butter
1 lb. fresh mushrooms
2 tsp. dried basil
½ tsp. oregano
½ tsp. seasoned salt
¼ tsp. garlic powder

Heat butter over medium high heat in a large skillet. Add mushrooms, cook until tender. Stir in basil, oregano, salt, and garlic powder. Reduce heat. Cover and cook 3–5 minutes longer.

Oven Fries .... *Susanna Kanagy*

4 large potatoes
¼ c. vegetable oil
1–2 Tbsp. Parmesan cheese
½ tsp. salt
¼ tsp. garlic powder
¼ tsp. paprika
⅛ tsp. pepper

Cut potatoes into wedges. Combine remaining ingredients and brush half over potatoes. Bake at 375° for 1 hour. Baste with remaining oil mixture halfway through baking time.
Yield: 6-8 servings.

Vegetables, Sides

Seasoned Potato Wedges........ *Tammy Yoder*

red potatoes
garlic clove, minced
olive oil
seasoned salt
parsley flakes
pepper

Cut potatoes into wedges. In a bowl, roll potatoes in garlic and olive oil. Place on a round pizza stone. Sprinkle with seasoned salt. Bake at 400° for 45–60 minutes. Before serving, sprinkle with pepper and parsley flakes.

Note: Makes a quick and easy side dish.

Santa Fe Roasted Potatoes....... *Renae Weaver*

2½ lb. red potatoes, scrubbed
1 Tbsp. garlic
1 tsp. oregano
1 tsp. chili powder
½ tsp. cumin
¼ tsp. pepper
½ tsp. salt
2 dashes cayenne pepper (optional)
¼ c. vegetable oil

Cut potatoes into 1" cubes. Place them in a greased 9"x13" baking pan. Combine the remaining ingredients. Pour over potatoes, toss to coat. Bake uncovered at 350° for 1 hour, stirring every 15 minutes.

Yield: 6 servings.

Topping for Baked Potatoes....... *Susan Miller*

¼ c. butter, softened
½ c. sour cream
2 Tbsp. chopped onions
1 c. shredded cheddar cheese

Mix butter and sour cream, then stir in onions and cheese.

Yield: approximately 1¾ cups.

Twice-Baked Potatoes .... *Sheryl Kanagy*

6 potatoes, washed
⅓ c. butter
2 tsp. salt
⅛ tsp. pepper
½ c. sour cream
½ c. milk
1½ c. shredded cheddar cheese or Velveeta cheese slices

Bake potatoes uncovered at 425° for 1 hour or until soft. Scoop out pulp, leaving the shell intact. Combine pulp, butter, salt, pepper, sour cream and milk. Whip till fluffy and light. Stuff shells with potato mixture. Cover and refrigerate. Bake at 425° for 20 minutes. Top with cheese the last 5 minutes.
Yield: 8 servings.

Candied Sweet Potatoes .... *Gina Mast*

5 med. sweet potatoes
1 tsp. salt
1 c. brown sugar
3 Tbsp. flour
2 Tbsp. butter
8 large marshmallows
½ c. chopped nuts (optional)
1 c. thin cream

Cook potatoes until tender; drain and cool. Cut lengthwise and arrange in greased dish. Mix salt, sugar, and flour. Pour over sweet potatoes. Dot with butter, marshmallows and nuts. Pour cream over all. Bake at 350° for 30 minutes.

Candied Sweet Potatoes .... *Fern Weaver*

6 sweet potatoes
1 c. brown sugar
1 c. mini marshmallows
½ c. butter
1 c. heavy cream

Cook and peel sweet potatoes. (Don't overcook.) Slice potatoes, and put in a greased 9"x13" pan. Sprinkle sugar on top. Cut butter in small pieces; dot across potatoes. Sprinkle with marshmallows and pour cream over all. Bake at 350° for 30–40 minutes.
Yield: 6 servings.

Brown Rice Casserole .... *Katie Stoltzfus*

1¼ c. uncooked rice
1 (10 oz.) can Campbell's beef broth
1 (10 oz.) can Campbell's consommé
1 sm. can mushrooms, sliced
1 soup can water
1 med. onion
½ c. butter or margarine

Put uncooked rice in 1½ quart casserole dish with broth, consommé, mushrooms with juice and water. Chop onion and brown with butter, pour into casserole.
Serves 10–12 people.

Herbed Rice Pilaf .... *Renae Weaver*

2 c. long grain rice
½ c. chopped onions
¼ c. butter
4 c. chicken broth
1 tsp. Worcestershire sauce
1 tsp. soy sauce
1 tsp. dried oregano

Combine all ingredients in a greased 2 quart baking dish. Bake covered at 350° for 50 minutes.
Yield: 8-10 servings.

*Let my words like vegetables, be tender and sweet,
for tomorrow I may have to eat them.*

Fried Tomatoes .... *Tammy Yoder*

4 large tomatoes
8 oz. cream cheese, softened
¼ c. fresh parsley, minced
1½ tsp. fresh basil or
   ½ tsp. dried basil
1 garlic clove, minced
¼ tsp. salt
¼ c. flour
1 c. bread crumbs
1 egg
1 Tbsp. milk
3 Tbsp. butter
3 Tbsp. olive oil

Cut each tomato into 4 thick slices, and place on paper towels to drain. In a small bowl, beat cream cheese, parsley, basil, garlic and salt until blended. Spread cream cheese mixture over 8 tomato slices, and top with remaining slices. Place flour and bread crumbs in separate bowls. In another bowl whisk egg and milk. Coat top and bottom of each sandwich with flour, dip in egg mixture, then in crumbs. Fry over medium-high heat for 3–4 minutes on each side or until golden brown. Drain on paper towels. Serve immediately.
Yield: 8 servings.

Fried Tomatoes .... *Katie Stoltzfus*

4 med. tomatoes
½ c. flour
3 Tbsp. lard
½ tsp. salt
⅛ tsp. pepper
2 Tbsp. brown sugar
1 Tbsp. flour
1 c. cream

Use ripe but firm tomatoes. Do not remove skins. Cut in slices ⅓ inch thick. Roll in flour and fry in hot lard. When browned on both sides, sprinkle with salt, pepper and brown sugar. Place tomatoes on platter. Add flour to drippings; when well blended add the cream. Allow gravy to thicken, then pour it over the fried tomatoes.
Yield: 5 servings.

Squash Casserole .... Rachel Kanagy

2 c. yellow summer squash, cubed
1 c. bread cubes
½ c. milk
3 Tbsp. butter, melted
2 eggs
1 Tbsp. chopped onions
½ tsp. salt
¼ tsp. pepper
1 c. shredded cheddar cheese
3 slices bacon fried and crumbled

Cook squash in small amount of water until soft. Mix bread, milk, butter, eggs, onion, salt and pepper with squash. Put in casserole dish. Top with cheese and bacon. Bake uncovered at 350° for 45 minutes.
Yield: 6 servings.

Squash Casserole .... Esther Stoltzfus

2 c. squash, cooked
2 c. cracker crumbs
2 eggs
1 c. diced onions
1 c. milk
1 c. cheddar cheese
salt and pepper to taste

Mix all ingredients together. Pour in a greased 9"x13" pan. Bake at 350° for 1 hour or until set and golden brown.

Squash Casserole .... Fern Weaver

4 c. chopped squash, cooked
½ c. butter
1 lg. onion, chopped
2 c. cubed cheese
1 Tbsp. sugar
2 eggs, beaten
salt and pepper to taste
2 c. crushed soda crackers
Velveeta cheese

Mix all ingredients except Velveeta together, put in casserole dish or 9"x13" pan. Bake at 325° for 45 minutes or until lightly browned. Put Velveeta cheese on top and let melt.
Yield: 12 servings.

Zucchini Fritters .... *Elsie Yoder*

vegetable oil
½ c. milk
1 egg, lightly beaten
1 c. flour
1½ tsp. baking powder
½ pkg. (1 oz.) ranch dip mix
2 c. shredded zucchini

Fill a deep-fat fryer or skillet with oil to a 2" depth. Heat to 375°. Meanwhile, combine milk and egg in a mixing bowl. Stir together dry ingredients and add to egg mixture, blend well. Fold in zucchini. Drop batter by rounded teaspoonfuls into hot oil. Fry until deep golden brown, turning once. Drain thoroughly on paper towels.
Yield: 1–1½ dozen.

The value of anything is what the next day's memory of it shall be.

A Taste of Blackville

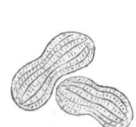

Cakes, Cheesecakes, and Frostings

Recipe featured on previous page:
Mocha Cake *page 145*

Blueberry Cake .... *Lori Miller*

1 c. butter
2 c. sugar
3 eggs
3 c. flour
1½ tsp. baking powder
⅛ tsp. salt
½ c. milk
1 tsp. vanilla
2 c. blueberries, fresh or frozen
2 tsp. sugar
2 tsp. flour

Glaze:

1¼ c. powdered sugar
1 tsp. vanilla
1–3 tsp. milk

Mix butter sugar and eggs till fluffy. Mix dry ingredients together and add, alternating with milk. Add vanilla. Coat blueberries with sugar and flour. Fold into batter. Pour into a greased bundt pan. Bake at 350° for 70–80 minutes. Mix glaze ingredients together and glaze cake while still a little warm.
Note: Very good, tastes like a pound cake.

Carrot Cake .... *Alta Miller*

2 c. sugar
4 eggs
1½ c. vegetable oil
1 tsp. vanilla
2 tsp. cinnamon
½ tsp. salt
2 tsp. soda
2 c. flour
3 c. shredded carrots
1 c. chopped nuts

Icing:

8 oz. cream cheese
½ c. butter
1 tsp. vanilla
1 lb. powdered sugar
dash of salt

Cream sugar and eggs, then add remaining ingredients, stirring in carrots and nuts last. Bake at 350° until toothpick comes out clean. Can be baked in 3 round cake pans or a 9"x13" pan. Mix icing ingredients together and frost cake.
Yield: 16-20 servings.

Cocoa Cake Roll .... *LaVerda Weaver*

3 eggs, separated
½ c. sugar
½ c. flour
⅓ c. cocoa
⅓ c. sugar
½ tsp. soda
¼ tsp. salt
⅓ c. water
1 tsp. vanilla

Peanut Butter Whipped Cream Filling:

1 c. Reese's peanut butter chips
⅓ c. milk
1½ c. miniature marshmallows
1 c. heavy whipping cream
1 tsp. vanilla

Line 10"x15" jelly-roll pan with aluminum foil; grease foil generously. Beat egg yolks and add ½ cup sugar, continue beating 2 minutes. In separate bowl, combine dry ingredients and add to yolk mixture alternately with vanilla and water. Beat on low till batter is smooth. Beat egg whites till foamy, then add 1 tablespoon sugar and beat till stiff peaks form. Carefully fold into chocolate mixture. Spread batter in pan. Bake at 375° for 15-18 minutes. Invert onto slightly dampened towel, remove foil and immediately roll up from narrow end. Let set 1 minute. Unroll and remove towel. Re-roll cake and cool completely. Then fill with peanut butter whipped cream filling. You may glaze with a chocolate frosting.

Peanut Butter Whipped Cream Filling: Melt peanut butter chips, milk and marshmallows over medium heat, cool to lukewarm. Whip cream until stiff. Fold in vanilla and peanut butter mixture.

Chocolate Ice Cream Roll ..... *LaVerda Weaver*

¼ c. sifted cake flour
½ tsp. salt
¼ c. cocoa
1 c. powdered sugar
5 eggs, separated
1 tsp. vanilla
1 quart vanilla ice cream

Grease a 11"x16" jelly-roll pan, and line with wax paper. Then grease wax paper too. Mix flour, salt, cocoa and sugar. Beat egg yolks till thick and yellow colored. Beat egg whites until stiff and add vanilla. Fold egg yolks into egg whites, then carefully fold in dry ingredients. Spread in pan and bake for 15–20 minutes at 400°. Turn out on a towel, remove paper, and starting with short side, roll up in the towel and let cool. Unroll and spread with ice cream. Re-roll cake and wrap in wax paper. Put in freezer till you serve it.

Chocolate Lover's Chocolate Cake ......
Elsie Yoder

1 Duncan Hines devil's food cake mix
1¾ c. milk
2 eggs
1 (3.4 oz) box chocolate instant pudding
1 (12 oz.) Nestle's chocolate morsels

Mix together cake mix, milk, eggs, and pudding. Stir in chocolate morsels. Bake 40–45 minutes at 350° in greased and floured Bundt pan. Cool slightly and empty onto plate.

Note: I like to serve this warm with ice cream and strawberries.

Yield: 12 servings.

Chocolate Peanut Butter Cupcakes
Fannie Mae Kanagy

¾ c. creamy peanut butter
¼ c. powdered sugar
2½ c. all-purpose flour
⅓ c. cocoa
1½ tsp. baking soda
½ tsp. salt
¾ c. butter, softened
1 c. sugar
3 eggs, room temperature
4 oz. chocolate chips, melted and cooled
1 c. buttermilk
2 tsp. vanilla

Frosting:

4 oz. cream cheese, softened
4 Tbsp. butter, softened
⅓ c. creamy peanut butter
1¼ c. powdered sugar, sifted

Preheat oven to 350°. Grease 2 (12 cup) muffin tins, or line with cupcake papers. Combine peanut butter and powdered sugar. Beat until light and fluffy. Whisk flour, cocoa, soda, and salt together in medium bowl. Combine butter and sugar. Beat till light and fluffy at medium speed. Beat in eggs, one at a time. Pour in melted chocolate and beat till thoroughly combined, about 30 seconds. Add flour mixture and buttermilk alternately to butter mixture and beat to combine. Add vanilla. Fill muffin tins half full with batter. Spoon ½ tablespoon peanut butter mixture on top. Don't spread. Spoon remaining batter over peanut butter. Bake 18–20 minutes, or until top springs back when touched. The normal toothpick test for doneness won't work due to the filling. Remove from oven and cool completely.

Frosting: Beat first three ingredients at medium speed until creamy, about 3 minutes. Add powdered sugar and beat till light and fluffy, about 2 minutes. Frost tops of cupcakes.

Yield: 24 cupcakes.

Hershey Almond Cake .... *Susan Miller*

1 chocolate cake mix
8 oz. cream cheese
1 c. powdered sugar
½ c. sugar
12 oz. Cool Whip
6 (1.55 oz) Hershey bars with almonds, divided

Prepare cake mix according to directions on box. Bake in 3 round cake pans. Beat cream cheese, then add powdered sugar and sugar. Chop 5 candy bars, then fold cream cheese mixture and candy bars into Cool Whip. Put icing between layers and on top and sides of cake. Chop remaining candy bar and garnish top and sides.

Hot Fudge Pudding Cake .... *Tammy Yoder*

1 c. sugar, divided
1 c. flour
7 Tbsp. cocoa, divided
2 tsp. baking powder
¼ tsp. salt
½ c. milk
⅓ c. butter, melted
1½ tsp. vanilla
½ c. brown sugar, packed
1¼ c. hot water

In a bowl stir together ½ cup sugar, flour, 3 tablespoons cocoa, baking powder and salt. Blend in milk, butter and vanilla; beat until smooth. Pour batter into 8" or 9" square pan. In a separate bowl, stir together remaining ½ cup sugar, brown sugar and remaining 4 tablespoons cocoa; sprinkle evenly over batter. Pour hot water over top, do not stir. Bake at 350° for 35-40 minutes or until center is almost set. Let stand 15 minutes before serving.

Lemon Cream Cheese Pound Cake......
Renae Weaver

2½ c. sugar
1¼ c. butter
6 oz. cream cheese
5 eggs
¾ tsp. lemon flavoring
2⅔ c. flour
⅜ tsp. salt

Glaze:

powdered sugar
milk
lemon flavoring

Cream sugar, butter, and cream cheese together for 10 minutes. Add eggs and flavoring and beat for 15 minutes. Add flour and salt. and beat for 5–10 minutes. Put into a greased and sugared bundt pan. Bake at 350° for 50–60 minutes.
Glaze: Combine ingredients to form a thin glaze.
Yield: 12 servings.

Pound Cake........................*Lill Stoltzfus*

1 c. butter
½ c. Crisco
5 lg. eggs
3 c. sugar
3 c. flour
⅛ tsp. salt
½ tsp. baking powder
1 c. sweet milk
2 Tbsp. rum flavoring

Blend butter and Crisco. Add eggs alternately with sugar and beat till light in color. Measure flour by using tablespoon to put into cup. Add flour, salt, and baking powder alternately with milk. Add flavoring last. Bake in bundt pan at 325° for 75–90 minutes.
Note: This is Alvin's favorite dessert.

Mayonnaise Cake..................*Alta Miller*

3 c. flour
6 Tbsp. cocoa
3 tsp. soda
1½ c. sugar
1½ c. mayonnaise
1½ c. water
1 tsp. vanilla

Mix dry ingredients. Add mayonnaise, water and vanilla and beat well. Bake in greased 9"x13" pan or jelly-roll pan. Bake at 350° till toothpick inserted comes out clean.
Note: This works very well for Mocha Cake. See page 145.
Yield: 15 servings.

Mocha Cake....................... *Alta Miller*

1 chocolate cake baked in a jelly-roll pan

Filling:

12 oz. cream cheese
½ c. butter, softened
3 c. whipped whip-n-ice
1 Tbsp. instant coffee, dissolved in a little water
1 tsp. vanilla
3 c. powdered sugar

Icing:

1 c. chocolate chips
½ c. butter
1 Tbsp. Karo syrup

Bake chocolate cake of your choice. Cut in thirds crosswise.
Filling: Beat cream cheese, then add butter and whip-n-ice. Beat. Add remaining filling ingredients and mix well. Put filling between layers of cake.
Icing: Melt chocolate chips and butter over low heat. Stir in Karo syrup. Put warm icing on top of cake and allow it to run down over edges. Refrigerate before serving.
Note: Whip-n-ice can be found at some bulk food stores.
Yield: 12-16 servings.

Pumpkin Cake .... *Lori Miller*

4 eggs
2 c. sugar
1 c. vegetable oil
2 c. flour
2 tsp. baking soda
2 tsp. cinnamon
½ tsp. salt
1 tsp. vanilla
2 c. pumpkin

Frosting:

6 oz. cream cheese
¾ c. powdered sugar
1 c. chopped nuts
½ c. butter
1 tsp. vanilla

Combine eggs and sugar, beat well. Add rest of ingredients and beat well. Bake at 350° for 1 hour. Cool. Mix frosting ingredients and spread on cake. Cake should be refrigerated.

Shortcake .... *LaVerda Weaver*

½ c. shortening
1½ c. sugar
2 eggs
1 tsp. vanilla
2¼ c. flour
3 tsp. baking powder
1 tsp. salt
1 c. milk

Mix in order given and spread batter in a 9"x13" baking pan. Bake at 350° for 25-30 minutes. Enjoy with strawberries and milk or Cool Whip.

Shortcake .... *Sheryl Kanagy*

½ c. butter, softened
1 c. sugar
2 eggs
1 tsp. vanilla
½ tsp. salt
½ tsp. baking soda
1¼ tsp. baking powder
2½ c. flour
1 c. milk

Preheat oven to 345°. Cream butter, sugar, eggs, and vanilla well. Add remaining ingredients and mix well. Pour batter into a greased 9"x13" pan and bake at 345° for 25–30 minutes. Serve warm with fresh strawberries and milk.
Yield: 6-8 servings.

It is not generous, it is merely right, to give others credit for what they do or try to do.

Swiss Roll Cake .... Valetta Yoder

2 c. flour
2 c. sugar
¾ c. cocoa
2 tsp. baking powder
1 tsp. baking soda
½ tsp. salt
2 eggs
1 c. sour cream
1 c. vegetable oil
2 tsp. vanilla
1 c. hot coffee

Filling:

8 oz. cream cheese
8 oz. Cool Whip
1 c. powdered sugar

Topping:

1½–2 c. chocolate chips
½ c. butter

Mix together cake ingredients, adding coffee last. Batter will be thin. Line on 11"x15" pan with greased wax paper. Spread batter in pan. Bake at 350° for 20–25 minutes. Invert onto towel. Remove wax paper. Immediately roll cake with towel. Cool. Beat filling ingredients together. Unroll cake and spread filling on top of cake. Re-roll. Melt chocolate chips and butter together and drizzle on top of cake roll.

Caramel Frosting .... Gina Mast

½ c. butter
1 Tbsp. brown sugar
⅓ c. milk
1 Tbsp. vanilla
3 c. powdered sugar
  (approximately)

Melt butter in saucepan. Add brown sugar and boil 1 minute. Add milk and bring to a boil. Remove from heat and add vanilla. Cool to room temperature. Add powdered sugar to desired consistency.

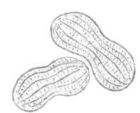

Glaze .... Susan Miller

4½ Tbsp. butter
6 Tbsp. milk
¾ c. sugar
1½ c. powdered sugar
½ tsp. vanilla
dash of salt

Boil first three ingredients for 2–3 minutes. Remove from heat and stir in powdered sugar, vanilla, and salt.

Note: This is great for cookies, soft pretzels, turnovers, cinnamon rolls, etc.

Cheesecake .... Lill Stoltzfus

Crust 1:

2½ c. graham cracker crumbs
½ c. butter, melted
¼ c. brown sugar

Crust 2:

2½ c. crushed Oreo cookies
½ c. butter, melted
¼ c. white sugar

Filling:

24 oz. cream cheese, softened
1 c. sugar
2 c. sour cream
4 eggs
1 tsp. vanilla
1 Tbsp. lemon juice

Crust: Make either crust 1 or crust 2. Mix and pack in cheesecake pan.

Filling: Beat cream cheese and sugar till smooth, add sour cream and eggs (1 at a time, beating after each one.) Add vanilla and lemon juice. Pour in pan and bake at 300° for 40–45 minutes.

Note: For variation, stir instant coffee in after cheesecake is in pan. Melt chocolate chips and mix with 1 cup filling and swirl. Flour 1½ cup raspberries and gently place in filling.

De Lime in De Coconut Cheesecake.....
Susan Miller

Crust:
1 c. graham cracker crumbs
½ c. coconut, sweetened and shredded
3 Tbsp. butter, melted
3 Tbsp. sugar
1 tsp. lime zest, grated

Filing:
32 oz. cream cheese
4 eggs
1 tsp. vanilla
½ c. sour cream
¼ c. fresh lime juice
1 (15 oz.) can sweetened cream of coconut milk

Preheat oven to 325°. Combine all crust ingredients. Blend in food processor just until blended. Press in bottom of 10" Springform pan.

Filling: Beat cream cheese until smooth. Then add eggs one at a time. Beat well. Add remaining ingredients and beat. Pour into crust. Bake 75–90 minutes, or until center jiggles slightly. Run knife around inside of pan. Cool to room temperature, then cover and refrigerate overnight. May be garnished with whipped cream and lime wedges.

Yield: 16 servings.

Peanut Butter Cheesecake...... *Glenda Weaver*

Crust:
1 pkg. Oreos
4 Tbsp. butter, melted

Filling:
12 oz. cream cheese
3 c. powdered sugar (scant)
1¼ c. peanut butter
24 oz. Cool Whip

Crush cookies and stir in butter. Press in 9"x13" pan and bake at 350° for 3 minutes. Cool. Beat cream cheese until smooth. Add powdered sugar, peanut butter, and Cool Whip. Pour over cooled crust.

Yield: 15 servings.

Rhubarb Cheesecake............Susan Miller

1 c. plus 1 Tbsp. flour
1¼ c. sugar, divided
½ c. butter
3 c. diced rhubarb
12 oz. cream cheese
2 eggs

Topping:
1 c. sour cream
2 Tbsp. sugar
1 tsp. vanilla

Combine 1 cup flour, ¼ cup sugar and butter; press in medium springform pan. Combine rhubarb, ½ cup sugar and 1 tablespoon flour and spread over crust. Bake at 375° for 15 minutes. Beat cream cheese, ½ cup sugar and 2 eggs and pour over hot rhubarb mixture. Bake at 350° for 30 minutes longer. Mix topping ingredients, and spread over top. Bake 5 more minutes if desired.
Yield: 16 servings.

Frozen Mocha Cheesecake.... Esther Stoltzfus

Oreos
2 tsp. instant coffee, heaping
1 Tbsp. hot water
16 oz. cream cheese
1 can sweetened condensed milk
½ c. chocolate syrup
8 oz. Cool Whip

Crush Oreos and put in bottom of 9"x13" pan. Dissolve coffee in hot water and set aside. Mix together cream cheese, sweetened condensed milk, and chocolate syrup. Add coffee and Cool Whip. Pour over crust. Garnish with a few crushed Oreos. Freeze.

Cookies, Bars, Candies

Recipe featured on previous page:

Chocolate Chip Cookies *page 155 (top)*

Black Raspberry Coconut Thumbprints
Valetta Yoder

½ c. butter
½ c. Crisco
¾ c. sugar
1 c. brown sugar
1 tsp. vanilla
2 eggs
¼ c. water (scant)
1 tsp. salt
1 tsp. baking soda
3½ c. flour
1 c. coconut
Black raspberry jelly, warmed

Cream butter, Crisco and sugars about 2 minutes. Add vanilla and eggs; beat well. Stir in water. Add the dry ingredients; mix well. Form into balls and roll into coconut. Bake at 350° for 12 minutes. Remove from oven and make small indentation in cookie; fill with jam. Return to oven and bake 1–2 minutes longer.

Cake Mix Cookies
Gina Mast

2 boxes yellow cake mix
⅔ c. butter
2 eggs
¼ c. water
1–2 c. chocolate chips

Mix all ingredients together. Drop by teaspoonfuls onto cookie sheet. Bake at 375° for 8–10 minutes.

The way to worry about nothing is to pray for everything.

Chocolate Marshmallow Cookies........
Elsie Yoder

1¾ c. flour
½ tsp. baking soda
½ tsp. salt
½ c. cocoa
½ c. shortening
1 c. sugar
1 egg
½ c. chopped pecans
1 tsp. vanilla
18 marshmallows, cut in half
36 pecan halves

Cocoa Frosting:

2 c. powdered sugar
5 Tbsp. cocoa
dash of salt
3 Tbsp. butter, melted
¼ c. light cream
½ tsp. vanilla

Sift flour with soda, salt and cocoa. Cream shortening. Add sugar gradually, blending thoroughly; add egg, and beat well. Add flour mixture and milk alternately, beating after each addition. Add chopped nuts and vanilla; mix. Drop mixture by teaspoonfuls about 2" apart onto well greased cookie sheet. Cookies will spread. Bake in 350° oven for 8 minutes. Top with marshmallow half, cut side down. Return to oven and bake 2 minutes until marshmallow softens. Cool and frost with cocoa frosting. Top with pecan halves.

Frosting: Sift powdered sugar with cocoa and salt. Add melted butter, cream and vanilla. Beat until smooth and creamy. Spread on cookies.

Chewy Chocolate Chip Cookies *Lori Miller*

1½ c. butter, softened
1¼ c. sugar
1¼ c. brown sugar, packed
2 eggs
1 Tbsp. vanilla
4¼ c. flour
1 tsp. baking powder
1 tsp. baking soda
1 tsp. salt
2 c. chocolate chips

Combine butter, sugar and brown sugar. Beat till creamy. Add eggs and vanilla. Continue beating till well mixed. Gradually add dry ingredients. Stir in chocolate chips. Bake at 350° for 10 minutes or till lightly golden brown. Do not overbake.

Yield: 4 dozen

Chocolate Chip Cookies .... Ruth Weaver

2½ c. all-purpose flour
1 tsp. baking soda
½ tsp. salt
½ c. butter or margarine
½ c. shortening
1 c. brown sugar, packed
½ c. sugar
2 eggs
1½ tsp. vanilla
2 c. chocolate chips

Stir together flour, soda and salt. In a separate bowl, beat butter and shortening. Add sugars and beat till fluffy. Add eggs and vanilla, beat well. Add dry ingredients to beaten mixture, beating till well combined. Stir in chocolate chips. Drop by teaspoonfuls onto an ungreased cookie sheet. Bake at 375° for 8–10 minutes or till done.
Yield: 5 dozen.

Chocolate Chip Cookies .... Fern Weaver

1½ c. butter
1½ c. sugar
1½ c. brown sugar
3 eggs
¼ c. peanut butter
2 tsp. vanilla
¾ tsp. salt
3 tsp. soda
4½ c. flour
1 (12 oz.) bag chocolate chips

Cream butter and sugars. Add eggs, beat well. Add remaining ingredients. Drop by teaspoonfuls onto cookie sheet and bake 12 minutes at 325°.
Yield: 6 dozen.

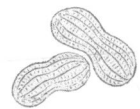

Chocolate Magic Cookies . . . . *Valetta Yoder*

¾ c. butter
1 c. sugar
⅔ c. brown sugar
2 eggs
2 tsp. vanilla
1 tsp. baking soda
½ tsp. salt
2 c. flour
⅔ c. cocoa
1 tsp. espresso powder
16 oreos, crushed
9 (fun sized) almond joy mounds, chopped
1½ c. chocolate chips

Cream butter and sugars together. Mix in eggs. Beat in vanilla, soda and salt. Add flour, cocoa, and espresso powder. Stir in oreos, candy bars and chocolate chips. Chill 30 minutes. Bake at 350° for 12 minutes.

Luscious Carrot Cookies . . . . *Elsie Yoder*

¾ c. sugar
1 c. butter
1 c. cooked carrots, mashed
1 tsp. vanilla
1 egg
2 c. flour
2 tsp. baking powder
½ tsp. salt

Icing:

3 Tbsp. butter, melted
2 Tbsp. orange juice
⅛ tsp. salt
powdered sugar

Cream sugar and butter together. Add mashed carrots, vanilla, and egg; mix well. Sift dry ingredients together and add to creamed mixture. Drop by teaspoonfuls onto lightly greased baking sheet. Bake at 350° for 15 minutes. Frost with orange flavored icing.
Icing: Mix butter, juice and salt, add powdered sugar; beat until creamy and spreading consistency.

Mattie Cookies (Butterscotch) *Katie Stoltzfus*

7 c. flour
2 tsp. baking soda
2 tsp. cream of tartar
1 tsp. salt
1 c. butter
1 c. shortening
4 c. brown sugar
4 eggs
2 tsp. vanilla
1 c. chopped pecans (optional)

Sift together dry ingredients. Mix butter, shortening, and brown sugar well. Add the eggs, vanilla, and nuts. Add flour mixture to creamed mixture. Fold all together. Drop on greased cookie sheet. Bake at 350° for 8–10 minutes.

Molasses Raisin Cookies.... *Fannie Mae Kanagy*

2 lb. raisins
3½ lb. flour
3½ c. sugar
1 tsp. salt
1 lb. shortening or butter
5 eggs, beaten
1 pt. mild molasses
3 Tbsp. soda
½ c. boiling water

Boil raisins in 1 cup water for 10 minutes; then cool. Mix flour, sugar, and salt. Cut in shortening like pie crust crumbs. Mix cooled raisins into crumbs. Add eggs and molasses. Pour boiling water over soda and add to raisin mixture. Mix well and chill dough. Form into long rolls 2" in diameter and wrap in plastic wrap and refrigerate or freeze. Cut into ½" slices and bake at 350° for 10–12 minutes.

Note: Rolls will keep in freezer a long time. Slice and bake as needed.

Yield: 15 dozen.

Molasses Crinkles .... *Rachel Kanagy*

¾ c. butter
1 c. brown sugar
1 egg
1 tsp. vanilla
6 Tbsp. molasses
2 tsp. baking soda
½ tsp. salt
1 tsp. cinnamon
½ tsp. ginger
2¼ c. flour
sugar

Cream butter and sugar together. Beat in egg, vanilla, and molasses. Add next 5 ingredients and mix well. Chill dough for 1–2 hours. Roll into balls and coat with sugar. Bake at 325° for 12 minutes. Do not overbake. Let set a few minutes on pan before removing.

Yield: 3 dozen.

Chewy Oatmeal Cookies .... *Renae Weaver*

2 c. brown sugar
1 c. vegetable oil
   or shortening
2 eggs
1 tsp. baking powder
1 tsp. baking soda
½ tsp. salt
1 tsp. vanilla
3 c. oatmeal
½ c. coconut
1½ c. flour
1–2 c. chocolate chips,
   (optional)
powdered sugar

Beat the first 3 ingredients together. Add the rest of the ingredients and mix well. Roll into balls. Roll balls in powdered sugar. Bake at 350° for 8–10 minutes.

Yield: 3 dozen.

Oatmeal Cookies .... *Sheryl Kanagy*

1 c. butter
2 c. brown sugar
2 eggs
1 tsp. vanilla
1½ c. flour
1 tsp. baking powder
1 tsp. baking soda
½ tsp. salt
3 c. oatmeal

Cream butter and brown sugar. Add eggs and vanilla; mix well. Add remaining ingredients. Chill dough 1 hour. Form into balls and roll in powdered sugar. Bake at 350° for 8–10 minutes.
Yield: 5 dozen.

Oatmeal Cranberry White Chocolate Cookies .... *Tammy Yoder*

⅔ c. butter, softened
⅔ c. brown sugar
2 large eggs
1½ c. old-fashioned oats
1½ c. flour
1 tsp. baking soda
½ tsp. salt
1¼ c. dried cranberries
⅔ c. white chocolate chips

Beat together butter and sugar until light and fluffy. Add eggs, mix well. Combine oats, flour, baking soda and salt in a separate bowl. Add to butter mixture in several additions, mixing well after each addition. Stir in cranberries and white chocolate chips. Drop by rounded teaspoonfuls onto ungreased cookie sheet. Bake for 10–12 minutes or until golden brown. Cool on wire rack.
Yield: 2½ dozen.

Ice Box Cookies .... *Lori Miller*

¾ c. butter
1 c. brown sugar
1 egg
2 c. flour
½ tsp. baking soda
½ tsp. cream of tartar
½ c. nuts
1 tsp. vanilla

Cream butter, sugar and egg. Add remaining ingredients. Shape into 1" rolls. Chill overnight. Slice and place on an ungreased baking sheet. Bake at 400° for 10–12 minutes.
Note: These are cookies my Grandma made at Christmas time.

Strawberry Cream Cookies .... *Lori Miller*

1 c. butter
1 c. sugar
3 oz. cream cheese
1 egg
1 Tbsp. vanilla
2½ c. flour
¼ tsp. salt
¼ tsp. baking powder
strawberry jam

Cream butter, sugar and cream cheese. Add egg and vanilla. Mix well. Add dry ingredients. Chill dough. Shape into 1" balls and place on an ungreased baking sheet. Make an indentation in the center of each cookie. Fill each indentation with ½ teaspoon jam. Bake at 350° for 12–15 minutes. Drizzle with icing of your choice.

Note: These are nice tea party cookies.

Vermont Maple Cookies .... *Lori Miller*

½ c. shortening
1 c. brown sugar, packed
2 eggs
1 c. sour cream
1 Tbsp. maple flavoring
2¾ c. flour
½ tsp. baking soda
1 tsp. salt
1 c. chopped nuts (optional)

Maple Butter Glaze:

½ c. butter
2 c. powdered sugar
2 tsp. maple flavoring
4 oz. cream cheese

Mix shortening, sugar and eggs thoroughly. Stir in sour cream, and maple flavoring. Stir together flour, soda and salt; blend in. Mix in nuts. Chill dough if soft. Bake at 375° for 10 minutes. If desired, spread cooled cookies with maple butter glaze.

Glaze: Heat butter until golden brown. Blend in powdered sugar, flavoring and cream cheese.

White Chocolate Snickerdoodles
Valetta Yoder

1 c. butter
1½ c. sugar
2 eggs
1 tsp. vanilla
2¾ c. flour
2 tsp. cream of tartar
1 tsp. baking soda
½ tsp. salt
2 c. white chocolate chips
2 Tbsp. sugar
2 tsp. cinnamon

Cream butter, sugar and eggs together. Add vanilla. Mix in flour, cream of tartar, soda and salt. Add white chocolate chips. Mix together sugar and cinnamon. Form dough into balls and roll in sugar and cinnamon mixture. Bake at 350° for 10 minutes.

Blueberry Bars
LaVerda Weaver

1 c. butter
1¾ c. sugar
4 eggs
3 c. flour
1½ tsp. baking powder
1 tsp. salt
2 c. (16 oz.) blueberry pie filling

Glaze:

1½ c. powdered sugar
1½ tsp. butter
2–3 Tbsp. milk

Mix first 6 ingredients. Put half of batter on sheet cake pan. Take a spoon and dollop filling over batter. Then put remaining batter on top. Take knife and swirl. Bake at 350° till done. Drizzle with glaze.

Note: I use a little more glaze.

Caramel and Chocolate Pecan Bars......
Lori Miller

2 c. flour
1 c. brown sugar, packed
½ c. butter
1 c. pecan halves
⅔ c. butter
½ c. brown sugar, packed
1 c. chocolate chips

Mix together first 3 ingredients until mixture resembles fine crumbs. Press onto bottom of ungreased 9"x13" pan. Place pecans evenly over unbaked crust. Combine ⅔ cup butter and ½ cup brown sugar in a saucepan. Cook over medium heat, stirring constantly until it comes to a full boil. Cook for 1 minute stirring constantly. Pour mixture evenly over pecans and crust. Bake for 18–22 minutes. Do not over bake! Immediately sprinkle with chips. Allow chips to melt slightly, then swirl melted chips over bars.

Note: You can use a combination of your favorite nuts or baking chips for variety in these bars.

Chocolate Chip Bars .... *Renae Weaver*

3 c. brown sugar
1⅓ c. vegetable oil
4 eggs
2 tsp. vanilla
3 c. flour
2 tsp. baking powder
2 tsp. salt
1½ c. chocolate chips

Combine sugar, oil, and eggs. Add vanilla and dry ingredients. Mix well. Stir in chocolate chips. Put into greased cookie sheet. Batter will be fairly stiff. Bake at 350° for 25 minutes.

Yield: 24 bars.

Ultimate Chocolate Chip Cookie and Fudge Brownie Bar .... *Valetta Yoder*

1 c. butter, softened
1 c. sugar
¾ c. brown sugar
2 eggs
1 Tbsp. vanilla
2½ c. flour
1 tsp. baking soda
1 tsp. salt
2 c. chocolate chips
1 pkg. double-stuffed Oreos
1 box brownie mix
¼ c. hot fudge topping

Cream butter and sugars together on medium speed for 3–5 minutes. Add eggs and vanilla; mix well. Slowly add flour, soda and salt until just combined. Stir in chocolate chips. Line a 9"x13" pan with wax paper and spray with cooking spray. Spread cookie dough in pan. Top with a layer of oreos. Mix brownie mix, according to package directions, adding ¼ cup hot fudge topping to the mix. Pour over oreos. Bake at 350° for 45–55 minutes.

Chocolate Raspberry Crumb Bars ....
LaVerda Weaver and Amy Swartzentruber

1 c. butter, softened
½ c. brown sugar, packed
2 c. flour
¼ tsp. salt
2 c. chocolate chips, divided
1 (14 oz.) can sweetened condensed milk
⅓ c. seedless raspberry jam
½ c. chopped nuts (optional)

Beat butter till creamy. Beat in brown sugar, flour and salt until crumbly. Press 1¾ cups crumb mixture onto bottom of greased 9"x13" baking pan. Reserve remaining crumbs. Bake at 350° for 10–12 minutes or until edges are golden brown. In small saucepan, combine 1 cup chocolate chips and milk. Cook over low heat stirring until smooth. Spread over hot crust. If desired stir nuts into remaining crumbs; sprinkle over chocolate filling. Drop teaspoonfuls of jam over crumb mixture. Sprinkle with remaining chocolate chips. Bake at 350° for 25–30 minutes.
Yield: 3 dozen.

Cream Cheese Brownies ...... *Susanna Kanagy*

2 c. sugar
1 c. butter, melted
4 eggs
1 tsp. vanilla
1 c. flour
¾ c. cocoa
½ tsp. baking powder

Filling:

8 oz. cream cheese, softened
1 egg
½ c. chocolate chips

Mix together sugar and butter with a wooden spoon. Beat in eggs and vanilla. Combine flour, cocoa and baking powder, stir into batter. Pour into greased 9"x13" pan. Beat together cream cheese and egg. Drop by spoonfuls over brownie batter. Swirl with a knife. Sprinkle with chocolate chips. Bake at 350° for 20–25 minutes.

Note: A 9"x13" size brownie mix may be used in place of brownie batter.

Yield: 12 servings.

Double Chocolate Bars .... *Glenda Weaver*

1½ c. flour
1 tsp. baking powder
1 tsp. salt
2 Tbsp. cocoa
2 c. sugar
1 c. vegetable oil
4 eggs
2 tsp. vanilla
2 c. chocolate chips

Combine dry ingredients; add oil, eggs and vanilla. Mix well. Fold in chocolate chips. Pour into a large cookie sheet. Bake at 350° for 25 minutes. Do not overbake.

Frosted Peanut Butter Fingers . . . . . . *Fern Weaver*

1 c. butter, softened
1½ c. brown sugar
1 c. sugar
2½ c. creamy peanut butter, divided
1 egg
1½ tsp. vanilla
2½ c. quick oats
2 c. flour
1 tsp. baking soda
½ tsp. salt

Frosting:

½ c. butter
½ c. cocoa
⅓ c. milk
1 tsp. vanilla
4 c. powdered sugar

Cream butter and sugars; add 1 cup peanut butter, egg and vanilla. Mix well. Add next 4 dry ingredients. Mix well and spread on greased cookie sheet, bake at 350° for 15 minutes. Cool slightly, spread remaining 1½ cup peanut butter on top. Cool completely, then put frosting on top and cut in squares.

Frosting: Cook butter, cocoa and milk for 1–2 minutes. Remove from heat; add vanilla and powdered sugar. Spread on top of peanut butter.

Lemony Raisin Bars . . . . *Alta Miller*

Filling:

2 c. raisins
1 (14 oz.) can sweetened condensed milk
1 Tbsp. lemon juice
1 Tbsp. grated lemon rind

Crust:

1 c. butter, softened
¾ c. brown sugar, packed
1½ tsp. vanilla
1 c. flour
½ tsp. baking soda
¼ tsp. salt
2½ c. quick oats
1 c. chopped pecans or walnuts

Filling: In saucepan, combine raisins, sweetened condensed milk, lemon juice and rind. Cook and stir over medium heat just till bubbly. Cool slightly. In a separate bowl, combine butter, brown sugar and vanilla, beat well. Add flour, baking soda and salt. Mix well. Stir in oats and nuts. Reserve 2 cups crust mixture. Press remainder in 9"x13" pan. Spread raisin mixture over crust to ½" from edges. Sprinkle with reserved crust mixture, press slightly. Bake at 375° for 25–30 minutes or until golden brown.
Yield: 24 servings.

Date Bars
Edna Raber

1 c. sugar
1 c. brown sugar
1 c. butter
4½ c. flour
1 c. chopped pecans
¼ c. boiling water
1 Tbsp. baking soda
1 c. chopped dates
1 c. cane or dark Karo syrup
3 eggs, divided

Make crumbs with sugars, butter, and flour. Add pecans. In a separate bowl, pour boiling water over baking soda; add dates. Beat 2 eggs. Add eggs and syrup. Mix crumbs with date mixture. Dough will be thick. Spread on 13"x18" baking sheet. Beat remaining egg and brush top. Bake at 350° for 15 minutes, then at 325° for 25-30 minutes.
Note: This was Eli's mother's recipe.
Yield: 48 servings.

Deluxe Chocolate Marshmallow Bars
Sheryl Kanagy

¾ c. butter
1½ c. sugar
3 eggs
1 tsp. vanilla
1⅓ c. all-purpose flour
½ tsp. baking powder
½ tsp. salt
3 Tbsp. baking cocoa
½ c. chopped nuts (optional)
4 c. mini marshmallows

Topping:

1⅓ c. chocolate chips
3 Tbsp. butter
1 c. peanut butter
2 c. Rice Krispies

Cream butter and sugar. Add eggs and vanilla; beat until fluffy. Combine flour, baking powder, salt and cocoa; add to creamed mixture. Stir in nuts if desired. Spread into greased jelly-roll pan. Bake at 350° for 15–18 minutes. Sprinkle marshmallows evenly over cake. Return to oven for 2–3 minutes. Using a knife dipped in water, spread melted marshmallows evenly over cake; cool.
Topping: Combine chocolate chips, butter and peanut butter in a small saucepan. Cook over low heat, stirring constantly until melted and well blended. Remove from heat. Stir in cereal, and spread over bars. Chill.
Yield: 3 dozen.

Marble Squares
Lill Stoltzfus

- 1½ c. sugar
- 1½ c. brown sugar
- 1½ c. shortening or ¾ c. margarine and ¾ c. lard
- 4 eggs
- 2 tsp. baking soda
- 2 tsp. salt
- 2 tsp. vanilla
- 4 c. flour
- 2 (12 oz.) pkg. chocolate chips

Beat sugars and shortening until creamy. Add eggs and beat until creamy. Add next 4 dry ingredients. Spread into greased 9"x13" pan. Sprinkle chocolate chips on top. After baking 7 minutes, use knife and swirl melted chips into dough. Continue baking another 20 minutes or when dough turns light brown. Do not overbake.

Note: This recipe can also be made into chocolate chip cookies. The bars are very chocolaty! Adjust chocolate chips to taste.

Monster Bars
LaVerda Weaver and Amy Swatzentruber

- 1 c. butter
- 1 c. brown sugar
- 1 c. sugar
- 1½ c. peanut butter
- 3 eggs
- 1 tsp. vanilla
- 2 tsp. baking soda
- 4½ c. oatmeal
- 1 (12 oz.) pkg. chocolate chips
- 1 (12 oz.) pkg. M&M's

Mix ingredients in order given. Press into a greased 13"x18" jelly-roll pan. Bake at 350° for 15 minutes. Do not overbake.

Peaches N' Cream Bars

Elsie Yoder and Valetta Yoder

1 (8 oz.) tube crescent rolls
8 oz. cream cheese, softened
½ c. sugar
¼ tsp. almond extract
1 (21 oz.) can peach pie filling
½ c. all-purpose flour
¼ c. brown sugar, packed
3 Tbsp. cold butter
½ c. sliced almonds

Unroll crescent roll dough into one long rectangle. Press onto the bottom and slightly up the sides of a greased 9"x13" baking pan; seal perforations. Bake at 375° for 5 minutes. Cool completely on a wire rack. In a mixing bowl, beat the cream cheese, sugar and extract until smooth. Spread over the crust. Spoon pie filling over cream cheese layer. In a bowl, combine flour and brown sugar. Cut in butter until mixture resembles coarse crumbs. Stir in nuts; sprinkle over peach filling. Bake at 375° for 25–28 minutes. Yield: 2 dozen bars.

A little girl came home with a box of dirt and cautioned her mother to be very careful with it. "What is it?" Her mother asked. "It's instant mud pies," said the budding homemaker.

Peanut Butter Chocolate Chip and Pretzel Squares .... Amy Swatzentruber

Crust:

- ¾ c. butter, softened
- 1 c. brown sugar
- ½ c. sugar
- 2 large eggs
- 2 tsp. vanilla
- 2 c. all-purpose flour
- 1 tsp. baking soda
- ½ tsp. salt
- 1–2 c. chocolate chunks or chips
- 1½ c. mini pretzel twists, coarsely broken, divided
- ¼ c. peanut butter
- ¼ c. chocolate chips

Preheat oven to 350°. Beat butter and sugars until fluffy. Beat in the eggs and vanilla. Add the flour, baking soda, and salt. Stir until almost combined. Add the chocolate chips and 1 cup of the pretzel pieces and stir until just blended. Spread the batter evenly in a 9"x13" pan and bake for 20–25 minutes or until golden. In a small bowl, melt the peanut butter and chocolate chips, stirring until smooth. Sprinkle the bars with the remaining crushed pretzel pieces and drizzle with peanut butter-chocolate mixture. Let cool until set.

Peanut Butter Dream Bars .... Lori Miller

Crust:

- 2 c. oatmeal
- 1½ c. flour
- 1 c. brown sugar
- 1 tsp. baking soda
- ¾ tsp. salt
- 1 c. butter, melted

Toppings:

- ⅓ c. peanut butter
- 1–2 cans sweetened condensed milk
- 1 c. chocolate chips

Mix oatmeal, flour, sugar, soda and salt. Add butter. Mix till it becomes crumbly. Reserve 1½ cup crumbs. Press rest of crumbs in a 10"x15" pan. Bake at 375° for 12 minutes.

Topping: Combine peanut butter and milk. Spread over partially baked crust. Sprinkle chocolate chips and reserved crumbs on top. Bake for 20 minutes.

Note: Can also add mini M&M's if desired.

Pumpkin Pie Squares .... *Amy Swartzentruber*

Crust:
1 box yellow cake mix
½ c. butter, melted
1 egg, beaten

Filling:
3 c. (30 oz.) cooked pumpkin
3 eggs
½ c. brown sugar
¼ c. sugar
⅔ c. milk
1½ tsp. cinnamon

Topping:
1 c. reserved cake mix
½ c. sugar
½ c. cold butter
½ c. chopped nuts (optional)

Remove one cup of cake mix; set aside. Mix crust ingredients and press into bottom of a 9"x13" pan. Blend filling ingredients together and pour on top of crust. Mix topping and sprinkle on top of filling. Don't mix the topping too long or the butter will get too soft and not crumbly. Bake at 350° for 50–60 minutes.

Reese's Pieces Bars .... *Ruth Weaver*

1 c. butter
1 c. sugar
1 c. brown sugar
2 eggs
⅔ c. peanut butter
1 tsp. vanilla
2 c. flour
1 tsp. baking soda
½ tsp. salt
2 c. quick oats
1 c. chocolate chips

Frosting:
¾ c. powdered sugar
¾ c. peanut butter
4–6 Tbsp. milk

Mix butter, sugars, eggs, peanut butter and vanilla. Add flour, soda, salt and quick oats, mix well. Spread into greased 10"x15" baking pan. Bake at 350° for 20–25 minutes. Remove from oven and immediately sprinkle with 1 cup chocolate chips. Let stand 3 minutes. Spread. Cool. Mix frosting ingredients. Spread frosting on cooled bars.

Sour Cream Raisin Bars ..... *Fannie Mae Kanagy*

Crust:
1 c. brown sugar
1 c. butter
1¾ c. old fashioned oats
1¾ c. all-purpose flour
1 tsp. baking soda

Filling:
2 c. raisins
1½ c. water
3 egg yolks
1 c. sugar
1½ c. sour cream
2½ Tbsp. cornstarch
½ tsp. cinnamon
1 tsp. vanilla

Crust: Combine brown sugar, butter, oats, flour, and soda. Mix well. Press half the mixture on the bottom of a greased 9" x 13" pan. Bake 7 minutes, until partially cooked.

Filling: Combine raisins and water in medium saucepan. Cook over medium heat for 10 minutes. Drain well and set aside to cool. Combine egg yolks, sugar, sour cream, cornstarch and cinnamon in medium saucepan and stir till cornstarch is dissolved. Cook over medium heat until mixture thickens and resembles pudding, about 8 minutes. Remove from heat. Stir in raisins and vanilla. Pour onto crust. Crumble remaining oat mixture evenly over top. Bake at 350° for 25 minutes or until set. Cool completely before cutting.

Yield: 36 bars.

Tri-Level Brownies .... *Rachel Kanagy*

Layer 1:

1 c. flour
1 c. brown sugar
¾ c. butter, melted
2 c. oatmeal
½ tsp. baking soda
½ tsp. salt

Layer 2:

10 Tbsp. butter
1½ c. sugar
2 eggs
6 Tbsp. cocoa
½ c. milk
2 tsp. vanilla
½ tsp. salt
½ tsp. baking powder
1½ c. flour

Layer 3:

2¼ c. powdered sugar
¼ c. cocoa
¼ c. butter
1 tsp. vanilla
3–4 Tbsp. milk

Layer 1: Mix all ingredients together and press into a well-greased 11"x15" baking sheet. Bake at 350° for 7 minutes.

Layer 2: Cream butter and sugar. Add eggs, cocoa, milk and vanilla and mix well. Add remaining ingredients and mix until moistened. Spread over crust and bake at 350° for 20 minutes. Let bars cool.

Layer 3: Mix ingredients together and frost cooled bars.

Yield: 20–24 servings.

Almond Toffee Candy.............*Susan Miller*

2 c. sliced almonds
11 oz. milk chocolate, grated
1 c. butter
1 c. sugar
3 Tbsp. cold water

Bake almonds at 350° until browned, stirring occasionally. Put 1 cup almonds on bottom of greased jelly-roll pan. Place half of chocolate on top of almonds. Cook butter, sugar and water to soft crack. Pour over almonds and chocolate. Immediately place remaining chocolate on hot mixture, then top with remaining almonds. When cooled, break into pieces.

Homemade Gumdrops............ *Gina Mast*

2½ c. sugar, divided
1⅓ c. applesauce
2 (3 oz.) pkg. flavored Jell-O
2 envelopes unflavored gelatin
1 tsp. lemon juice

In a large saucepan, combine 2 cups sugar, applesauce, flavored Jell-O, unflavored gelatin, and lemon juice; let stand for 1 minute. Bring to a boil over medium heat, stirring constantly. Boil for 1 minute. Immediately pour into a cold 11"x7" baking dish coated with cooking spray. Refrigerate for 3 hours or until firm. With a spatula, loosen gelatin from sides of pan. To remove, invert onto waxed paper. Using kitchen scissors, or small sharp cookie cutters dipped in hot water, cut into 1" squares or shapes. Place on waxed paper. Dry at room temperature for about 8 hours or until slightly sticky. Roll in the remaining sugar. Store in airtight container.

Peanut Butter S'mores .... *Marisa Weaver*

1 Tbsp. peanut butter
1 med. flour tortilla
2 Tbsp. milk chocolate chips
¼ c. mini marshmallows

Spread peanut butter over tortilla. Sprinkle remaining ingredients over top. Microwave 45 seconds. Allow to cool 3–5 minutes. Roll jelly-roll style when cool.

Note: For variation, substitute grated carrots, apples, raisins, bananas or crushed pineapple for chocolate chips and marshmallows.

Desserts

Recipe featured on previous page:
Strawberry Brownie Trifle *page 184*

Apple Strudel .... Lill Stoltzfus

Dough:
- 2½ c. flour
- 2 Tbsp. sugar
- ½ tsp. salt
- 1 c. butter
- 2 egg yolks
- milk

Filling:
- 4–5 apples, peeled and diced
- 1 Tbsp. milk
- 1 Tbsp. flour
- ⅔ c. brown sugar
- ½ tsp. cinnamon

Glaze:
- 1 c. powdered sugar
- 1 tsp. vanilla
- 1 Tbsp. butter
- water

Dough: Cut dry ingredients into butter. Beat egg yolks in a measuring cup. Fill to ½ cup with milk. Mix into dry ingredients, like as for pie crust. Divide dough in half. Press half into 9"x13" pan.

Filling: Stir ingredients together. Spread filling mixture over crust. Roll other half of dough to fit over the filling. Press to seal edges. Prick or make holes in top. Bake at 350° for 50 minutes.

Glaze: Combine powdered sugar, vanilla, and butter. Add water to desired consistency. Drizzle over top.

Caramel Dumplings .... Lori Miller

Dough:
- 1 c. flour
- 1 tsp. baking powder
- ⅛ tsp. salt
- 3 Tbsp. sugar
- 3 Tbsp. butter
- ½ tsp. vanilla
- ½ c. milk

Syrup:
- 1 c. brown sugar
- 1 c. water
- 2 Tbsp. butter

Dough: Work first five ingredients together like pie crust, then add vanilla and milk.

Syrup: In a saucepan. Combine ingredients and boil for 3 minutes. Pour syrup in baking pan and drop dumplings on top. Bake at 350° for 20 minutes. Serve warm with ice cream.

Note: This is a recipe my Grandma used to make a long time ago.

Caramel Pudding .... Susan Miller

2 c. sugar
2 tsp. salt
⅔ c. flour
1 c. cream
3 c. milk
4 egg yolks, beaten
1 tsp. vanilla
4 tsp. butter

Mix sugar, salt and flour. Add cream. Heat milk, then add cream mixture and stir till thick. Remove from heat and add egg yolks, vanilla, and butter. Cool.

Note: This is very good to use for date pudding.

Chocolate Lasagna .... Ruth Weaver

1 pkg. Oreo cookies
6 Tbsp. butter, melted
8 oz. cream cheese
2 Tbsp. cold milk
¼ c. sugar
12 oz. Cool Whip, divided
2 pkg. instant chocolate pudding
3¼ c. cold milk
1½ c. mini chocolate chips

Crush Oreos and mix with butter. Press in a 9"x13" pan. Put in refrigerator. Mix cream cheese till light and fluffy. Add 2 tablespoons milk and sugar. Mix well. Stir in 1¼ cup Cool Whip. Spread over crust. In a bowl, combine pudding and 3¼ cup milk. Spread over cream cheese. Spread remaining Cool Whip over top. Sprinkle with chocolate chips and place in freezer for 1 hour or refrigerate 4 hours before serving.

Creamy Fruit Tapioca .... Rachel Kanagy

½ c. pearl tapioca
4 c. water
⅔ c. sugar
3 oz. strawberry Jell-O
20 oz. pineapple tidbits
2 c. whipped topping

Combine dry tapioca, water and sugar in a saucepan. Bring to a boil, then turn to low heat and cook until tapioca turns clear, about 20 minutes. Add Jell-O, and stir until dissolved. Cool. Stir in pineapple and chill thoroughly. Fold in whipped topping.

Note: you may also choose other fruit and Jell-O that complement each other.

Date Pudding .... *Elsie Yoder*

1 c. boiling water
1 c. chopped dates
1 c. sugar
1 tsp. baking soda
1 Tbsp. butter
1 egg
1 c. flour
½ c. chopped nuts

Pour boiling water over dates, add sugar, soda and butter. Cool. Mash with potato masher. Add egg, flour, and nuts. Mix well. Pour into a 9"x9" pan. Bake at 350° for 45 minutes or until set. Cool. Crumble and serve with layers of whipped cream and butterscotch sauce (see next recipe).

Butterscotch Sauce .... *Elsie Yoder*

½ c. brown sugar
3 Tbsp. boiling water
1 Tbsp. butter
½ tsp. salt
⅛ tsp. baking soda
⅓ c. flour
½ c. sugar
1½ c. boiling water
1 egg yolk
½ tsp. vanilla

Combine brown sugar, 3 tablespoons boiling water, butter and salt. When mixture begins to boil, add soda. Boil until syrup forms a hard ball in cold water. Combine flour and sugar; slowly add boiling water. Add first mixture to second and bring to a boil. Beat egg yolk, add ½ cup hot mixture to beaten yolk. Blend well, then add to remaining mixture and bring to a boil. Add vanilla. Cool. Use for date pudding.

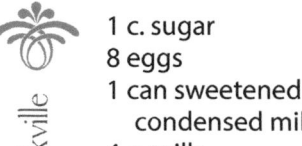

Flan .... *Valetta Yoder*

1 c. sugar
8 eggs
1 can sweetened condensed milk
4 c. milk
1 tsp. vanilla

Burn 1 cup sugar, pour into custard pan, coating all sides. Beat eggs well. Add rest of ingredients and blend well. Pour this mixture over syrup mixture in a custard pan. Place pan into another pan with warm water in it. Bake at 350° for 1 hour. Allow flan to cool, then refrigerate for several hours. Before serving turn upside down on a plate. The syrup will be on top.

Note: To burn sugar, place in a small kettle and turn burner to low heat. The sugar will be caramelized.

Yield: 8-10 servings.

Frozen Mocha Torte .... *Susanna Kanagy*

1¼ c. crushed Oreos
2 Tbsp. butter, melted
8 oz. cream cheese
1 can sweetened condensed milk
½ c. chocolate syrup
1½ Tbsp. instant coffee
1 Tbsp. hot water
8 oz. whipped topping

Combine 1 cup cookie crumbs and butter. Press into 9"x13" pan. Beat cream cheese, milk and syrup. Dissolve coffee in hot water and add to cream cheese mixture. Fold in whipped topping. Pour into 9"x13" pan. Sprinkle with remaining ¼ cup cookie crumbs. Freeze 8 hours.

Yield: 12 servings.

Fruit Pizza .... Lill Stoltzfus

Crust:

1 c. powdered sugar
1 c. sugar
1 c. butter
1 c. vegetable oil
2 eggs
2 tsp. vanilla
1 tsp. salt
1 tsp. baking soda
1 tsp. cream of tartar
5 c. flour

Topping for 1 pizza:

8 oz. cream cheese
1½ c. powdered sugar
1 tsp. vanilla
2 c. whipped cream
fruit of your choice

Glaze:

1 c. orange juice
½ c. sugar
clear jel to thicken

Cream sugars, butter, and oil till light and fluffy. Add eggs and vanilla. Sift dry ingredients together. Add and mix well. Spread in 3 pizza pans. Bake 15–20 minutes at 350° or until light brown. Cool. Beat together topping ingredients. Spread on cooled crust. Arrange fruit on topping. Combine glaze ingredients in saucepan and cook until thickened. Cool. Drizzle glaze over top of fruit. Really decorate it and add mint leaves or drizzle with chocolate.

Note: This crust recipe makes 3 pizza pans of crust. Can just make 1 crust and form the the rest into balls. Roll in sugar. Flatten with glass to make sugar cookies. This was Jamie's favorite dessert as a child.

Lemon Chiffon Pudding .... Valetta Yoder

1 c. sugar
¼ c. flour
¼ tsp. salt
3 Tbsp. butter
¼ c. lemon juice
grated rind of ½ lemon
3 eggs, separated
1 c. milk

Combine sugar, flour, salt and butter. Add lemon juice and rind and beaten egg yolks. Beat until ingredients are thoroughly blended. Add milk and blend the mixture. Beat egg whites until stiff. Fold in. Pour into a greased 8" x 8" baking dish and set in a pan of warm water. Bake at 350° for 45 minutes. Serve warm.

Mocha Dessert .... *Gina Mast*

18 oz. pkg. Oreo cookies
3 Tbsp. butter
3 Tbsp. instant coffee granules, heaping
3 c. milk
2 boxes instant chocolate pudding
16 oz. Cool Whip, divided

Crush Oreo cookies. Melt butter and mix with cookies. Save 1 cup and set aside. Press remaining cookies into a 9"x13" pan. Mix coffee, milk and pudding and add 1 cup Cool Whip. Spread on top of crust. Chill for 1 hour, then spread remaining Cool Whip on top of pudding. Sprinkle with 1 cup cookies.

Oreo Ice Cream Dessert .... *Fern Weaver*

1 pkg. Oreo cookies
¼ c. butter
½ gallon ice cream
16 oz. Cool Whip
chocolate syrup
peanuts (optional)

Crush cookies and mix with butter. Save 1 cup of crumbs for the top. Press the rest in a 9"x13" pan. Mix ice cream and Cool Whip, put on crumbs, Drizzle chocolate syrup over top. Put the rest of crumbs on top and freeze. Yield: 10 servings.

Pumpkin Pie Squares .... *Ruth Weaver*

Crust:

1 c. flour
1 c. oatmeal
½ c. brown sugar
½ c. butter

Topping:

2 c. pumpkin
2 c. milk
3 eggs, beaten
¾ c. sugar
½ tsp. ginger
2 tsp. cinnamon
½ tsp. salt
¼ tsp. cloves

Mix crust ingredients together until crumbly. Press into a 9"x13" pan. Bake at 350° for 12 minutes. Mix together topping ingredients and pour on top of crust. Bake 30 minutes longer or until set. Cool. Cut into squares. Serve with whipped topping or ice cream.

Pumpkin Torte .... Alta Miller

Crust:
½ c. sugar
½ c. butter, melted
2½ c. graham crackers crumbs

Cream Cheese Filling:
8 oz. cream cheese
2 eggs, beaten
¾ c. sugar

Pumpkin Filling:
1 pkg. Knox gelatin
¼ c. water
3 eggs, separated
1 c. sugar, divided
1 (15 oz.) can pumpkin
½ c. milk
½ tsp. salt
1 Tbsp. cinnamon
8 oz. Cool Whip for topping

Mix crust ingredients and press in bottom of 9"x13" pan.
Cream Cheese Filling: Beat together cream cheese, eggs and sugar. Spread over crust and bake 15 minutes at 350°. Cool.
Pumpkin Filling: Dissolve gelatin in water. Set aside. In saucepan, combine 3 egg yolks, ½ cup sugar, pumpkin, milk, salt and cinnamon. Bring to a boil, then remove from heat and add gelatin. Cool. Beat 3 egg whites and ½ cup sugar. Fold into pumpkin mixture. Spread over cream cheese filling. Top with Cool Whip.
Yield: 15 servings.

The power of remembering may be a gift, but the power of forgetting is a blessing.

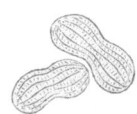

Reese's Pudding .... *Esther Stoltzfus*

Crust:

½ c. magarine
1 c. flour
½ c. sugar

Filling:

8 oz. cream cheese
1 c. powdered sugar
⅓ c. peanut butter
3 c. Cool Whip
3 c. milk
1 sm. box instant chocolate pudding
1 sm. box instant vanilla pudding
Cool Whip
Reese's cups to garnish

Crust: Mix all the ingredients and put in 9"x13" pan. Bake at 350° until brown. Cool.
Filling: Mix cream cheese, powdered sugar, peanut butter and cool whip together. Pour on to of crust. Mix milk and puddings. Pour over cream cheese mixture. Top with Cool Whip. Garnish with chopped Reese's cups.
Note: A graham cracker crust can also be substituted for the butter crust in this recipe.

Rhubarb Danish .... *Lori Miller*

4 c. chopped rhubarb
4½ c. water
2 c. sugar
½ c. tapioca
½ c. strawberry Jell-O

Cook rhubarb, water, sugar and tapioca till clear, then add Jell-O. Cool and enjoy!
Yield: 6-10 servings.

Strawberry Brownie Trifle .... *Renae Weaver*

1 pan brownies, cubed
2 qt. sliced strawberries
4 oz. cream cheese
¼ c. sugar
1½ c. whipped cream
1 box instant vanilla pudding
2 c. cold milk

Beat cream cheese and sugar until smooth. Fold in whipped cream. Combine pudding and milk and add to cream cheese mixture when set. Layer brownie pieces, white mixture, and sliced strawberries in a trifle bowl.
Yield: 12 servings.

Tapioca Pudding .... *Meagan Miller*

2 eggs, separated
4 c. milk, divided
⅔ c. sugar
⅛ tsp. salt
5 Tbsp. tapioca
3 Tbsp. sugar
1½ tsp. vanilla
8 oz. Cool Whip

Place egg yolks in a saucepan. Add ½ cup milk and blend well. Add ⅔ cup sugar, salt, tapioca and remaining milk. Bring to a boil. Meanwhile, beat egg whites till foamy. Add 3 tablespoons sugar slowly. Beat till soft peaks are formed. Pour into boiling mixture. Add vanilla and blend. Chill. When cooled, add Cool Whip.

Tiramisu Cheesecake Dessert *Susanna Kanagy*

1 (12 oz.) pkg. vanilla wafers
5 tsp. instant coffee, divided
3 Tbsp. hot water, divided
32 oz. cream cheese
1 c. sugar
1 c. sour cream
4 eggs, beaten
1 c. whipped topping
1 Tbsp. cocoa

Layer half of wafers in a 9"x13" pan. Dissolve 2 teaspoon coffee in 2 tablespoon hot water. Brush half over wafers. Beat cream cheese, sugar and sour cream. Add eggs just until combined. Divide batter in half. Dissolve remaining 3 teaspoons coffee in 1 tablespoon water. Stir into one part of batter. Spread over wafers. Layer with remaining wafers. Brush wafers with remaining coffee mixture. Top with remaining batter. Bake at 325° for 40–45 minutes or until almost set. Let cool and refrigerate overnight. Spread with whipped topping and sprinkle with cocoa. Yield: 12 servings.

Toffee Coffee Dessert .... *Renae Weaver*

15 Oreos, crushed
1¼ c. milk, divided
¼ c. sugar
1½ Tbsp. cornstarch
1 Tbsp instant coffee granules
1 Tbsp. butter
1 tsp. vanilla
1 can sweetened condensed milk
2 c. whipped cream
2 c. toffee bits

Place crushed Oreos in a 9"x13" pan, set aside. Bring 1 cup milk to a boil. Combine sugar, cornstarch, coffee, and remaining ¼ cup milk. Add to hot milk. Cook for 1 minute, until thickened. Remove from heat. Add butter and vanilla. Cool. Add sweetened condensed milk, whipped cream, and toffee bits. Pour over crushed Oreos. Freeze.
Yield: 15 servings.

Quickie Brownie Sundaes .... *Rachel Kanagy*

brownie mix (or your favorite brownie recipe)
vanilla ice cream
toppings of your choice

Mix brownies according to package directions. Put 2 tablespoons of batter into sundae cup or small glass bowl. Microwave for 30–40 seconds. Top with a scoop of ice cream and any desired fruit or sauce. They are delicious plain, too.
Note: this is great for impromptu company. The brownies turn out soft and fudgy in the microwave. Brownie batter keeps for a week in the refrigerator.

If we'd have more Mothers with the spirit of Mary, we'd have more sons with the Spirit of Jesus.

Dairy Queen Ice Cream ...... Susanna Kanagy

2 env. Knox gelatin
½ c. cold water
4 c. whole milk
2 c. sugar
2 tsp. vanilla
1 tsp. salt
3 c. cream

Dissolve gelatin in ½ cup cold water. Heat milk until hot, but not boiling. Remove from heat and add gelatin mixture, sugar, vanilla and salt. Cool and add cream. Refrigerate 5–6 hours or until completely chilled. Freeze in 4 quart ice cream freezer.
Yield: 1 gallon ice cream.

Homemade Ice Cream .... Gina Mast

3 qt. plus more milk
½ c. flour
½ c. cornstarch
6 eggs, separated
½ tsp. salt
3 c. sugar, divided
vanilla to taste
1 pt. cream

Bring 3 quarts milk to scalding. Combine flour, cornstarch, egg yolks, salt and ½ cup sugar. Add cold milk to make a thin paste. Pour the boiling milk into the mixture, stirring while you pour. This should get thick and smooth. Add 2 cups sugar. Beat the egg whites. Add egg whites and remaining ½ cup sugar alternately to mixture. Add vanilla and cream. Freeze.
Yield: 6 quarts ice cream.

Strawberry Ice Cream .... Glenda Weaver

½ c. sugar
2 c. strawberries, blended
1 can sweetened
   condensed milk
1 c. half and half
3 c. milk
¼ tsp. salt
½ Tbsp. vanilla

Mix together sugar and strawberries. Add rest of ingredients and mix well. Pour into a 4 quart ice cream freezer.

Butter Pecan Sauce ....Susan Miller

½ c. plus 2 Tbsp. brown sugar, packed
2 Tbsp. sugar
¼ c. cornstarch
¾ c. heavy whipping cream
1 Tbsp. butter
½ c. chopped pecans, toasted

Combine sugars and cornstarch. Gradually stir in cream until smooth. Bring to a boil over medium heat, stirring constantly. Cook and stir for 2–3 minutes or until slightly thickened. Remove from heat. Stir in butter until melted, then add toasted pecans.
Note: This is great drizzled over cheesecake or ice cream. Very rich!
Yield: 1½ cups.

Caramel Topping for Ice Cream ... Alta Miller

1½ c. brown sugar
⅔ c. light corn syrup
¼ c. butter
4 drops vinegar
½ c. cream

Combine sugar, syrup and butter in saucepan. Boil to 225° or soft ball. Remove from heat; add vinegar and cream.

Chocolate Topping for Ice Cream ... Alta Miller

1 c. sugar
⅓ c. cocoa
dash of salt
2 Tbsp. flour
1 c. milk
1 tsp. vanilla
1 tsp. butter

In saucepan, mix dry ingredients together. Gradually add milk and bring to a boil. Remove from heat and add vanilla and butter.
Note: Keeps in fridge at least a week.

Ice Cream Topping ....Renae Weaver

½ c. butter
1 c. chopped pecans
1 c. chocolate chips

Brown pecans in butter until dark brown. Pour into chocolate chips and stir until melted.
Yield: 8 servings.

Pies

Recipe featured on previous page:
Pecan Pie *page 194*

Pie Crusts............................ *Alta Miller*

4 c. flour
1½ c. lard
2 tsp. salt
1 egg, beaten
½ c. water
1 Tbsp. apple cider vinegar

Mix flour, lard and salt by hand till you have small crumbs. Mix egg, water and vinegar and gently mix with crumbs. Do not overmix. Divide into 6–8 balls, then roll out on floured surface with rolling pin.
Yield: 6-8 pie crusts.

Graham Cracker Crumb Crust............
Fannie Mae Kanagy

24 graham cracker squares
 or 1½ c. crumbs
¼ c. sugar
⅓ c. butter, melted

Combine crumbs, sugar and melted butter. Press onto the bottom and up sides of an ungreased 9" pie plate. Chill 30 minutes before filling or bake at 375° for 8–10 minutes, or until crust is lightly browned. Cool before filling.
Yield: 6 servings.

Joy is not the absence of trouble, but the presence of God.

Apple Cranberry Pie......... *Amy Swartzentruber*

2 pie crusts, unbaked or
    2 rolled refrigerated
    pie crusts
6 Granny Smith apples,
    peeled, cored, and sliced
½ c. cranberries
2 Tbsp. lemon juice
1¼ c. sugar
¼ c. all-purpose flour
1½ tsp. cinnamon
¼ tsp. allspice
⅛ tsp. salt
1 egg, beaten
1 Tbsp. whipping cream

Pastry Cream:

1 c. milk
¼ c. sugar
2 eggs yolks
3 Tbsp. sugar
3 Tbsp. cornstarch
¼ tsp. salt
2 Tbsp. butter
½ tsp. vanilla

Preheat oven to 375°. Roll out pastry on a floured work surface to a circle about 14" in diameter. Place in a 9" deep dish pie tin. Trim pastry edges even. In a large bowl, combine apples, cranberries, and lemon juice. In a small bowl combine sugar, flour, cinnamon, allspice and salt. Spread bottom of crust with pastry cream. Toss apple mixture with dry ingredients, pile over pastry cream in pie tin. Roll remaining pastry portion to 12" circle, place over apples. Trim to ½" beyond edge of pie tin. Fold top pastry under bottom pastry. Crimp edge as desired. Cut 4 small slits in top crust to allow steam to escape. Combine egg and cream; brush on pastry. Place on a foil-lined baking sheet. Bake 1 hour and 20 minutes. If necessary, cover edges of pie with foil to prevent over-browning. Cool on wire rack.

Yield: 10 servings.

Pastry Cream: In a small sauce pan combine milk and sugar. Cook over medium heat until bubbly on edges. Meanwhile, in medium mixing bowl beat egg yolks, sugar, cornstarch and salt until combined. Gradually beat in ⅓ cup hot milk mixture, quickly beat in remaining milk mixture. Return to saucepan; cook and stir over medium heat until mixture thickens and comes to a boil. Remove from heat. Stir in butter and vanilla. Cool. Can store in refrigerator up to 3 days.

Apple Crumb Pie .... *Alta Miller*

4 c. Granny Smith apples, coarsely chopped
½ c. brown sugar
½ c. sugar
1 tsp. cinnamon
¼ tsp. salt
2 Tbsp. flour, heaping
2 Tbsp. cream
1 Tbsp. butter
9" pie crust, unbaked

Crumbs:

¾ c. quick oats
¼ c. soft butter
¼ tsp. salt
½ tsp. baking soda
½ c. b. sugar
½ c. flour

Mix apples and all dry ingredients. Put in 9" unbaked pie shell. Drizzle cream over top, then dot with butter. Mix crumb ingredients to make crumbs, then put on top of pie. Bake at 425° for 15 minutes, then bake at 350° until apples are soft.

Yield: 6 servings.

Key Lime Pie .... *Valetta Yoder*

9" pie crust, baked
3 c. sweetened condensed milk
½ c. sour cream
¾ c. key lime juice
1 Tbsp. grated lime zest

Combine milk, sour cream, lime juice, and zest. Pour into crust. Bake at 350° for 8–10 minutes. Chill. Garnish with lime slices and whipped cream.

Easy Peach Cream Pie ...... *Fannie Mae Kanagy*

1½ lb. (3 c.) fresh peaches, peeled and sliced
9" pie shell, unbaked
2 eggs
1 c. sugar
¼ c. all-purpose flour
dash of salt
1 c. heavy cream
1 tsp. vanilla

Place peaches in unbaked pie shell. Beat eggs slightly in bowl, blend in sugar, flour and salt. Stir in cream and vanilla, blend well. Pour over peaches. Bake at 375° for 40–50 minutes or until center shakes slightly when moved. Serve warm or for firmer pie, chill before serving. Refrigerate any leftovers.

Note: To prevent crust edges from becoming too brown, cover edges with foil.

Yield: 8 servings.

Peach Cream Pie ... *Esther Stoltzfus and Lori Miller*

1 pie crust, unbaked
3-4 peaches, peeled and sliced
1 c. sugar
2 Tbsp. flour
1 egg
pinch of salt
1–1½ c. cream

Place sliced peaches in pie crust. Mix together sugar, flour, egg and salt. Add cream. Pour over sliced peaches. If pie crust is not full, more cream can be added. Bake at 350° for 45 minutes or until set.

Note: Lori says you can also add fresh raspberries.

Pecan Pie .... *Fannie Mae Kanagy*

1 pie crust, unbaked
1½ c. chopped pecans
3 eggs, slightly beaten
1 c. dark Karo syrup
½ c. sugar
1 Tbsp. butter
¼ tsp. salt
⅓ c. water
1½ Tbsp. flour
1 tsp. vanilla

Sprinkle pecans in bottom of pie crust. Mix remaining ingredients together and pour over pecans. Bake at 350° for 30–35 minutes. Serve with a dip of vanilla ice cream.

Pumpkin Pie .... *Fern Weaver*

2 pie crusts, unbaked
4 eggs
3 c. brown sugar
¼ c. flour
2 c. pumpkin
1 tsp. salt
4 c. milk
1½ tsp. cinnamon

Beat eggs until foamy, add six remaining ingredients. Pour into unbaked pie crusts. Bake at 400° for 15 minutes, then reduce heat to 350° for 40 minutes.
   Note: This recipe is from Mom Schrock. Mom always said to heat the milk before mixing in, to shorten the baking time.
   Yield: 2 pies.

Raisin Creme Pie .... *Alta Miller*

¾ c. raisins
⅓ c. water
¼ c. butter
¾ c. brown sugar
2 c. whole milk, divided
½ c. flour
1 egg yolk
1 tsp. vanilla
¼ tsp. salt
9" pie shell, baked
Cool Whip

Put raisins and water in saucepan, and bring to a boil. Simmer on low heat till water is absorbed. Set aside. Melt butter, add sugar, and stir till brown. Add 1½ cup milk and stir till sugar is dissolved. Make thickening with flour, egg yolk and remaining ½ cup milk. Add to butter/sugar mixture and bring to boil. Remove from heat and add salt, vanilla and raisins. Cool and pour into baked 9" pie shell. Top with Cool Whip.
   Yield: 6 people.

*We cannot direct the wind,
but we can adjust our sails.*

Raisin Crumb Pie .... *Alta Miller*

9" pie crust, unbaked

Filling:

½ c. raisins
1 c. brown sugar
2 Tbsp. cornstarch
2 c. water
1 Tbsp. vinegar
¼ tsp. salt

Crumbs:

1 c. flour
¼ c. shortening
½ c. brown sugar
½ tsp. baking soda

Place all filling ingredients except cornstarch in saucepan. Add just enough water to cornstarch to make a paste, then add to other ingredients. Bring to boil. Cool. Pour in unbaked 9" pie crust. Mix crumb ingredients into crumb consistency and place on top of filling. Bake at 425° for 5 minutes, then at 350° for 30 minutes.

Yield: 6 servings.

Southern Coconut Pie .... *Esther Stoltzfus*

1 pie shell, unbaked
3 eggs
1 c. sugar
½ tsp. salt
1 Tbsp. flour
3 Tbsp. soft butter
¾ c. milk
½ tsp. vanilla
1 c. coconut

Mix together eggs, sugar, salt and flour. Add the rest of the ingredients and pour into a pie shell. Sprinkle ½ cup coconut on top and bake at 325° for 1 hour.

Strawberry Pie .... *Fannie Mae Kanagy*

3½ c. water, divided
1 c. sugar
½ c. clear jel
1 (3 oz.) box strawberry Jell-O
dash of salt
dash of pepper
1½ qt. fresh strawberries, sliced
2 pie shells, baked
Cool Whip to garnish

Bring half of the water to a boil. Add sugar. Use remaining water to mix with clear jel. Add clear jel to boiling water and sugar. Cook till clear, stirring constantly. Add the Jell-O, salt, and pepper. Cool. Add strawberries and mix gently. Divide strawberry filling between 2 baked pie shells. Top with Cool Whip before serving.
Yield: 2 pies.

Strawberry Pie Filling Mix .... *Fern Weaver*

2 c. sugar
1 c. clear jel
2 pkg. strawberry Kool-Aid

Mix sugar, clear jel and Kool Aid. Place ¾ cup of mix and 2 cups cold water in a saucepan. Cook and stir until thick. Let cool. Add sliced strawberries for pie or delight.

Vanilla Crumb Pie .... *Elsie Yoder*

1½ c. sugar (scant)
4 c. water
2 eggs, beaten well
6 Tbsp. flour, heaping
1 c. Karo syrup
1 c. pancake or maple syrup
2 pie shells, unbaked

Crumbs:

2 c. flour
½ c. sugar
1 tsp. baking soda
½ tsp. cream of tartar
½ c. butter

Mix the first six ingredients together well. Heat on stove till boiling and thick. Pour into pie shells. Mix crumbs together and put over filling. Bake at 350° for 30 minutes.
Note: I like to make the filling the day before and refrigerate it.
Yield: 2 pies.

A Taste of Blackville

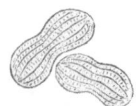

Canning & Freezing

Recipe featured on previous page:
Pickled Okra *page 203*

Apple Pie Filling . . . . *Edna Raber*

36 c. diced apples
8 c. sugar
¾ c. clear jel
½ c. fruit fresh

Mix sugar, clear jel and fruit fresh together. Add to diced apples. Put in quart containers and freeze. When adding to unbaked pie shell, dot apples with butter, sprinkle with a little cream and add top crust. Enough for 12 pies.
Note: This can also be canned. Add a vitamin C tablet on top of each quart to prevent browning. Cold pack pie filling for 15–20 minutes.
Yield: filling for 12 pies.

Canned Apple Pie Filling . . . . *Gina Mast*

5 c. water
5 c. sugar
½ tsp. cinnamon or to taste
¼ tsp. nutmeg
5 Tbsp. clear jel
7 qt. apples, peeled and chopped

Boil water, sugar, cinnamon and nutmeg for 5 minutes. Dissolve clear jel in a little water. Stir into boiling mixture. Pour over chopped apples and mix well. Put into jars. Hot water bath 15 minutes after it starts to boil.

Blackberry Jam . . . . *Rachel Kanagy*

7 c. sugar
5 c. blackberries, crushed
6 Tbsp. pectin

Measure sugar into a bowl. Put berries through a food mill to remove seeds. Mix berry pulp and pectin in a large kettle. Bring to a rolling boil. Add sugar quickly and mix. Bring back to a rolling boil, and boil for 1 minute. Ladle into jam jars. Hot water bath for 10 minutes.
Yield: 11 cups jam.

Fig Jam........................... *Fannie Mae Kanagy*

3 c. chopped figs
3 c. sugar
2 boxes strawberry or raspberry Jell-O

Mix and let set for 30 minutes. Boil 5 minutes. Put in jars and seal with lids.
Yield: 3 pints.

Frozen Strawberry Jam ... *Fannie Mae Kanagy, Fern Weaver, Gina Mast and Esther Stoltzfus*

8 c. chopped strawberries
16 c. sugar
1⅓ c. pectin mix
3 c. water

Mix sugar and strawberries and set aside for 40 minutes. Boil together pectin mix and water for 4 minutes, add to strawberries and stir until well mixed. Put in containers and let stand 24 hours at room temperature, then put in freezer.

Note: Esther lets strawberries and sugar set for 10 minutes and boils water and pectin for 1 minute.
Yield: 24–25 cups jam.

Dilly Beans...................... *Lill Stoltzfus*

2½ c. white vinegar
2½ c. water
¼ c. salt
green beans that have "gotten large"

Spice: (each pint)

1 tsp. cayenne pepper
4 garlic cloves
1 head dill

Boil first 3 ingredients. Pack beans upright in pint jar. Add all spice ingredients to each jar. Pour vinegar brine over beans. Seal jars. Boil 40 minutes.
Yield: 5 pints.

Pickled Okra .... *LaVerda Weaver*

okra
garlic

Brine:

2 c. vinegar
2 c. water
2 Tbsp. salt
2 Tbsp. dill seed

Pack okra in jars with one garlic clove per jar. Pour brine mixture over okra. Cook 5 minutes. Let set 1 month before opening.

Pickled Okra .... *Esther Stoltzfus*

3 lb. okra
3 c. water
3 c. vinegar
6 Tbsp. salt
dill seed

Wash and prick okra; put in pint jars. Add ½ teaspoon dill seed to every pint. Mix water, vinegar and salt. Pour over okra. Cold pack for 10 minutes.

Port Clinton Pickles .... *Lori Miller*

garlic cloves
fresh dill
hot banana peppers, halved
cucumbers
2 qt. white vinegar
2 qt. water
¾ c. coarse salt
1 c. sugar

In each quart jar; place 1 garlic clove, 1 head of fresh dill (or 1 teaspoon dill) and 1 hot banana pepper. Fill with cucumbers. Make a brine with vinegar, water, salt and sugar; bring to a boil, and pour over cucumbers. Cold pack approximately 5 minutes.
Yield: 9–10 quarts.

Sweet Dill Slices .... *Fannie Mae Kanagy*

7 garlic buds
4 dill heads
cucumbers
3 c. sugar
2 c. vinegar
2 c. water
2 Tbsp. salt
½ tsp. alum

Put 1 garlic bud and ½ head dill in each pint jar, slice cucumbers ½" thick into jars. Heat remaining ingredients to make syrup. Pour heated syrup over cucumbers in jars. Put on lids and cold pack with water in canner to cover jars. Bring to a boil; remove from heat. Remove canner lid, and let cool. They are ready to eat in 2 weeks.
Yield: 7 pints.

Freezer Cucumber Salad .... *Edna Raber*

2½ qt. shredded cucumbers
1 chopped onion
2 Tbsp. salt
1½ c. sugar
½ c. white vinegar

Mix cucumbers, onions, and salt; soak in refrigerator for 24 hours. Drain. Add sugar and vinegar. Soak another 24 hours. Put in containers and freeze.

Note: this is very refreshing especially during the winter.

Our limitations are God's opportunities.

Sauerkraut........................... *Lill Stoltzfus*

5 lb. cabbage
¼ c. salt
apple cider vinegar

Shred cabbage. Use either a crock, stainless steel bucket, or kettle to make sauerkraut. Pour enough vinegar in your container to cover the bottom. Add a layer of cabbage and some salt and firmly stomp, stomp, stomp until it is juicy. Repeat layers with remaining cabbage and salt. Cabbage should be covered with juice. Cover with cabbage leaves. Let set for two weeks. I do about 3–5 days on the counter, then I put it in the refrigerator. Put a plate over all to keep cabbage in juice. After two weeks, skim off top layer. Put in jars and boil for 30 minutes to seal.

Note: This recipe came from my grandma, Edna Falb. Happy New Year's Day!

Ketchup........................... *Lill Stoltzfus*

2 gal. tomato juice
½ c. salt
2 onions, shredded
¼ tsp. cinnamon oil
¼ tsp. clove oil
3 c. vinegar
8 c. sugar
6-8 Tbsp. clear jel

Put first 6 ingredients in a large kettle. Bring to a boil and simmer until volume is decreased by ⅓. Add sugar. Mix clear jel with a small amount of water. Add to mixture to thicken. Put in jars to seal.

Note: I like to use a food processor to shred the onions. This recipe was received from Martha Schrock. She said it was Wilbur's mom's recipe.

Pizza Sauce .... *Edna Raber*

2 gal. tomato juice
½ tsp. garlic salt
2 tsp. red pepper
5 green peppers, chopped
4 tsp. garlic powder
1 tsp. black pepper
4½ lb. onions, chopped
1½ c. vegetable oil
⅓ c. salt
1½ Tbsp. basil
¼ c. oregano
2 Tbsp. parsley flakes
1 Tbsp. Italian seasoning
3 bay leaves
3 (1.25 oz.) pkg. Italian spaghetti mix
2 c. sugar
48 oz. tomato paste
1 c. clear jel

In a large kettle, mix together first seven ingredients reserving 1 pint tomato juice. Cook for 1 hour, then add the rest of ingredients except clear jel. Cook 1 more hour. Mix clear jel with reserved tomato juice and add to the pizza sauce to thicken. Put into jars and process 15 minutes. Yield: 24 pints.

Pizza Sauce .... *Lori Miller*

8 celery ribs
9 onions
1 gal. tomato paste
9 qt. tomato juice
3 Tbsp. chili powder
6 Tbsp. salt
9 Tbsp. parsley flakes
6 Tbsp paprika
3 Tbsp. oregano
3 Tbsp. garlic powder
3 Tbsp. dry mustard
2 Tbsp. pepper
2 c. sugar
1 qt. ketchup
2½ c. Parmesan cheese

Coarsely chop celery and onions. Cook till soft. Put through blender. Put in large kettle. Add all remaining ingredients. Boil till throughly mixed. Pour into pint jars and cold pack for 20 minutes. Yield: 36 pints.

V-8 Juice .... *Ruth Weaver*

6 qt. tomato juice
¾ c. sugar
2 tsp. onion salt
2 tsp. celery salt
2 tsp. garlic salt
1 tsp. salt
½ tsp. pepper

Bring all ingredients to a boil. Put juice in quart jars. Pressure canner: Can with 5 pounds pressure for 10 minutes. Traditional: Cold pack for 10 minutes.

Note: You can use this juice in any recipe that calls for tomato juice. It makes delicious chili soup.

V-8 Tomato Juice ....
LaVerda Weaver, Fern Weaver and Gina Weaver

6 qt. tomato juice
⅔ c. sugar
1 tsp. garlic salt
2 tsp. celery salt
2 tsp. onion salt
2 Tbsp. salt

Heat everything, then put into jars. Put into canner and bring water to a boil. Boil for 20 minutes.

Note: Fern says sugar is optional.

Yield: 12 pints.

Tomato Soup .... Rachel Kanagy

6 qt. tomato chunks
3 onions
1 sm. bunch celery
1 jalapeño pepper (or to taste)
1½ c. sugar
3 Tbsp. salt
3 Tbsp. cornstarch
¾ c. butter

Clean and wash tomatoes. Cut into chunks. Do not peel. Cook until soft, put through food strainer to remove skin and seeds. Peel onions, clean celery and peppers and put in blender. Add tomato pulp until able to blend. Blend well. Put all vegetable pulp into a large kettle and bring to a boil. Mix sugar, salt and cornstarch together in a bowl. Stir into boiling liquid. Bring back to a boil. Add butter, stirring until melted. Ladle into pint or quart jars and hot water bath for 20 minutes.
Yield: 14 pints.

Deer Meat to Can .... Susanna Kanagy

deer meat, cut in 1" chunks

Seasonings:
(for each quart)

½ tsp. garlic salt
1 beef bouillon cube
1 tsp. vinegar
1 tsp. brown sugar

Fill quart jars with meat chunks. To each jar, add remaining ingredients. Fill jars ¾ full with water. Process at 10 pounds for 90 minutes, or cold pack for 3 hours. For pints, use half the amount of ingredients per jar and process at 10 pounds pressure for 70 minutes.

Canned Deer Chunks .... *Lori Miller*

deer meat, cut in chunks
1 tsp. onion soup mix
1 tsp. beef bouillon

Soak meat in vinegar and salt water for a few hours, Drain and fill pint jars to neck with chunks. Add seasonings and fill jar with water. Cold pack for 3 hours.

Note: You can use 2 teaspoon beefy onion soup mix instead of beef bouillon and the onion soup mix.

Cheese Sauce .... *Lori Miller*

½ c. butter
1 qt. milk
3–2 lb. boxes Velveeta cheese
3½ c. cream or 2 cans evaporated milk

Melt butter in pan and add milk. Heat. Add cheese in little chunks, and melt on low heat. Stir often so it doesn't burn. Pour into pint jars. Hot water bath for 20 minutes.

Note: I keep it in the refrigerator because it may unseal.

Yield: 12 pints.

A Taste of Blackville

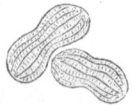

Miscellaneous

Recipe featured on previous page:

Boiled Peanuts *page 213*

Amish Mixed Peanut Butter.......*Renae Weaver*

½ c. light corn syrup
2½ c. brown sugar
2½ c. water
1 tsp. maple flavoring
3 lb. peanut butter
6 c. marshmallow creme

Combine corn syrup, brown sugar, water and flavoring. Bring to a boil. Cool. Add peanut butter and marshmallow creme. Mix well.
Yield: 15 cups.

Miscellaneous

Cinnamon Butter..................*Renae Weaver*

1 c. butter, softened
1 c. powdered sugar
2 Tbsp. honey
2 tsp. cinnamon

Whip all ingredients together and serve with warm rolls.
Yield: 20 servings.

Boiled Peanuts.....................*Lill Stoltzfus*

5 lb. peanuts
½ c. salt

Use fresh raw peanuts. Wash well, then put in kettle and cover with water. Add salt. Boil for at least 2 hours. If peanuts were drying out some, let set in water overnight to help soften them.

Cold Remedy....................*Glenda Weaver*

1 tsp. cinnamon
1 Tbsp. honey

Mix well and take 3 times a day as needed.

Cough Syrup....................*Glenda Weaver*

honey
onion

Cut up onion and pour equal amount of honey over it. Store in a jar. Take as often as needed.

Homemade Play Dough .... *Rachel Kanagy*

1 c. flour
½ c. salt
2 tsp. cream of tartar
1 Tbsp. vegetable oil
1 c. water
several drops food coloring

Mix flour, salt and cream of tartar in small kettle. Add oil and water. Stir and cook over medium heat until thick and ball is formed. Remove from kettle and knead several drops of food coloring into dough. Keep in airtight container.

Note: We loved when Mom would make this for us when we were young. She'd give us each a ball of dough and she'd let us knead and color our own.

Preserving Children.............. *LaVerda Weaver*

children
field
brook
dog
flowers

Take one large grassy field, one half dozen children all sizes. One dog, one long narrow strip of brook. Mix children with the other ingredients and empty them into the field, stirring continually. Sprinkle with field flowers. Pour brook gently over pebbles. Cover all with a deep blue sky and bake in a hot sun. When children are well browned, they may be removed and put in a bathtub to cool, with lots of soap and warm water.

Tupperware and Stainless Steel Cleaner...
Alta Miller

16 qt. warm water
½ c. lye
1 c. soap powder (Tide, etc.)
1 c. bleach

Dissolve lye in warm water. Add rest of ingredients. Soak approximately 5 minutes. Wash, rinse and dry.

Note: Take handles off of stainless steel before soaking.

Appetizers

Appetizer Cups 3
Cappuccino...........................13
Cauliflower Poppers....................3
Chai Tea Latte........................16
Cheese Ball 3
Christmas Party Pinwheels 4
Christmas Popcorn....................4
Coffee Party Punch...................14
Crab Crescent Loaf....................4
Créme de Menthe....................14
French Onion Hamburger Dip.........7
Fresh Fruit Dip........................5
Fresh Salsa............................5
Frozen Coffee Drink..................15
Fruit Sauce or Dip.....................5
Guacamole 6
Hamburger Dip 7
Hearty Calico Bean Dip................6
Hot Chocolate 14
Iced Coffee 14
Iced Coffee 15
Mexican Corn Dip.....................7
Mocha Shake 15
Party Deviled Eggs 8
Paul Harvey Punch 17
Pepperoni Rolls 8
Pico De Gallo 8
Pineapple Tea Drink..................17
Pizza Dip..............................9
Pretzel Dip............................9
Pumpkin Spice Latte 16
Sausage, Bean, and Spinach Dip 9
Seasoned Pretzels....................10
Seasoned Pretzels....................10
Smoky Bacon Wraps..................10
Southwestern Chicken Salad Spirals ..11
Spinach Dip..........................11
Strawberry Blender 18
Strawberry Daquiri...................18
Strawberry Pineapple Smoothie......18
Stuffed Mushrooms..................12
Sweet Little Smokies 11
Sweet Tea............................17
Taco Dip 12
Tomato and Bell Pepper Salsa 6
Tomato Bacon Cups..................12
Vegetable Dip 13
Vegetable Dip 13
Wedding Punch.....................19

Breads, Breakfast

Baked Oatmeal 44
Baked Oatmeal 44
Basic Crepes 27
Blueberry Coffee Cake................37
Breakfast Casserole 48
Brunch Pizza Cups 48
Butter Horns.........................23
Butter Horns.........................24
Challah Bread........................24
Cheese Fruit Braid 35
Cheesy Egg Grits.....................46
Chipa Guasú.........................28
Cinnamon Rolls.....................33
Coffee Cake..........................37
Coffee Cake..........................38
Cream Cheese Danish...............40
Dinner Rolls..........................25
Doughnuts 33
Easy Breakfast Pizza..................48
Easy Cinnamon Coffee Cake..........38
Easy Donuts 34
Easy Pancakes 42
Egg Bake 49
Flour Tortillas 28
French Bread 26
German Coffee Cake 39
Golden Garlic Bread..................28
Granola..............................45
Granola..............................46
Granola..............................45
Grits Casserole 47
Hash Brown Bake 49
Italian Bread Bowls...................27
Jalapeño Cheddar Bread 29
Lemon Blueberry Muffins 41
Lemon Poppy Seed Bread 32
Oatmeal Pancake Mix................43
Orange Twists.......................34
Overnight Sausage and Grits 47
Peanut Butter Granola...............46
Pecan Lemon Loaf 32
Pizza Crust...........................31
Pizza Hut Bread Sticks................29
Pizza Hut Bread Sticks................30
Pizza Hut Pizza Crust 31
Pumpkin Apple Muffins 41
Red Lobster Biscuits..................30
Scrambled Egg Muffins..............49
Skillet Cornbread 26
Soft Potato Rolls 25
Soft Pretzels 31
Southwest Sausage Bake.............50
Spinach Quiche......................50
Spinach Quiche......................51
Sticky Quickies.......................36
Stuffed French Toast 43
Swedish Tea Ring 36
Waffles 44
Wilbur Martha's Bread................23
Yellow Squash Muffins 42

Salads, Dressings

Bean and Barley Salad................55
BLT Salad 55
Broccoli and Pasta Salad.............59
Broccoli Cauliflower Salad...........56
Chicken and Black Bean Salad........56
Chinese Chicken Salad 57
Cole Slaw Dressing...................65
Cole Slaw 57
Cottage Cheese and
  Pineapple Salad 62
Cottage Cheese Jello Salad...........62
Cranberry Salad......................63
Cranberry Salad......................63
Dreamsicle Jell-O Salad 64
Easy Finger Jell-O 64
Festive Tossed Salad 58
Finger Jell-O 64
French Dressing 65
Honey Bacon Dressing 65
Italian Dressing 66
Marinated Tomato Salad 58
Pasta Salad 59
Pasta Salad 60
Poppy Seed Dressing..................66
Potato Salad 61
Potato Salad 60
Ramen Noodle Salad...................61
Southwest Chicken Salad..............62
Sweet and Sour Dressing..............67
Sweet and Sour Dressing..............66

Soups, Sandwiches

Barbecued Burgers....................77
Barbecue Sandwiches..................76
Beefy Bunwiches......................78
Catfish Stew 71
Cheddar and Bacon Burgers...........78
Chicken Salad........................79
Chili Soup 71
Chili Soup 72
Clam Chowder.........................72
Coney Sauce Chili for Hot Dogs 80
Creamy White Chili...................73
Creamy Wild Rice Soup................73
Grilled Cheese Sandwiches...........80
Ham Cheddar Chowder 74
Hot Chicken Salad 79
Mexican Shrimp Bisque 74
Mushroom Sausage Pizza Soup.........75
Pizza Sandwiches 80
Poppy Seed Sandwiches 81
Potato Soup 75
Sloppy Joes - large recipe 81
Sloppy Joes..........................81

Spinach Salad Wraps..................82
Stromboli............................82
Taco Soup 76
Three Ingredients Soup 76
Turkey Sandwiches....................83

Meats, Main Dishes

Alice Springs Chicken 87
Anna's Marinade 117
Baked Chicken in Mushroom Gravy 87
Baked Spaghetti 99
Barbecued Meatballs................ 100
Barbecued Meatballs................ 100
Barbecued Spareribs 101
Barbecue Sauce..................... 118
Beaufort Stew...................... 112
Belizean Rice and Beans
  with Ricardo Chicken 88
Black Eyed Peas with Ham 109
Burrito Casserole.................. 103
Caprese Chicken with Bacon..........89
Chicken Barbecue Marinade........ 118
Chicken Breasts over Pasta 89
Chicken Bundles 90
Chicken Delicious....................90
Chicken Enchiladas 91
Chicken Enchiladas 92
Chicken Enchiladas 91
Chicken Marinade................... 117
Chicken Marinade................... 118
Chicken Noodles......................93
Chicken Spaghetti Casserole 94
Creamy Chicken Enchiladas 92
Deep Dish Taco Squares............. 104
Egg Rolls............................93
Enchilada Casserole 101
Fettuccine Alfredo 113
Four-Cheese Chicken Fettuccine 94
Fried Empanadas 103
Garlic Beef Enchiladas............. 102
Glorified Texas Hash............... 107
Grilled Ham Marinade............... 119
Grilled Honey Bacon Fish........... 113
Herb Chicken 94
Japanese Chicken.....................95
Lime Honey Glazed Salmon 114
Mexican Dish 104
Mexican Lasagna.................... 105
Mini Cheddar Loaves................ 108
Pizza Rice 105
Popover Pizza...................... 107
Pork Roast 111
Potato Haystack Casserole.......... 109
Scalloped Potatoes with Ham
  large recipe 110
Scalloped Potatoes with Ham 110

Scrumptious Beef	112
Sesame Chicken	96
Shrimp and Grits	115
Shrimp and Grits	114
Shrimp and Rice Casserole	115
Shrimp and Wild Rice Casserole	117
Shrimp Scampi	116
Smoked Sausage Skillet	111
Sour Cream Chicken	97
Spicy Chicken Casserole	97
Steak Marinade	119
Stir Fry	116
Sweet and Sour Chicken	98
Sweet and Sour Chicken	98
Tortilla Stacks	106
Vietnam Fried Rice	106
Wrapped Venison Steak	112
Yummy Spaghetti	99
Zucchini Pizza Casserole	108

Vegetables, Sides

Baked Beans	123
Baked Corn Casserole	126
Baked Lemon Pasta	128
Baked Macaroni and Cheese	128
BBQ Green Beans	126
Broccoli Casserole	124
Broccoli Elegant	124
Brown Rice Casserole	132
California Blend Casserole	125
Candied Sweet Potatoes	131
Candied Sweet Potatoes	131
Colorful Veggies	125
Fried Mushrooms	129
Fried Tomatoes	133
Fried Tomatoes	133
Herbed Rice Pilaf	132
Hush Puppies	127
Mom's Baked Beans	123
Onion Rings	127
Oven Fries	129
Roasted Asparagus	123
Santa Fe Roasted Potatoes	130
Scalloped Corn	126
Seasoned Potato Wedges	130
Southern Macaroni Pie	129
Squash Casserole	134
Squash Casserole	134
Squash Casserole	134
Topping for Baked Potatoes	130
Twice-Baked Potatoes	131
Zucchini Fritters	135

Cakes, Cheesecakes, Frostings

Blueberry Cake	139
Caramel Frosting	147
Carrot Cake	139
Cheesecake	148
Chocolate Ice Cream Roll	141
Chocolate Lover's Chocolate Cake	141
Chocolate Peanut Butter Cupcakes	142
Cocoa Cake Roll	140
De Lime in De Coconut Cheesecake	149
Frozen Mocha Cheesecake	150
Glaze	148
Hershey Almond Cake	143
Hot Fudge Pudding Cake	143
Lemon Cream Cheese Pound Cake	144
Mayonnaise Cake	144
Mocha Cake	145
Peanut Butter Cheesecake	149
Pound Cake	144
Pumpkin Cake	145
Rhubarb Cheesecake	150
Shortcake	146
Shortcake	146
Swiss Roll Cake	147

Cookies, Bars, Candies

Almond Toffee Candy	173
Peanut Butter Chocolate Chip and Pretzel Squares	169
Black Raspberry Coconut Thumbprints	153
Blueberry Bars	161
Cake Mix Cookies	153
Caramel and Chocolate Pecan Bars	162
Chewy Chocolate Chip Cookies	154
Chewy Oatmeal Cookies	158
Chocolate Chip Bars	162
Chocolate Chip Cookies	155
Chocolate Chip Cookies	155
Chocolate Magic Cookies	156
Chocolate Marshmallow Cookies	154
Chocolate Raspberry Crumb Bars	163
Cream Cheese Brownies	164
Date Bars	166
Deluxe Chocolate Marshmallow Bars	166
Double Chocolate Bars	164
Frosted Peanut Butter Fingers	165
Homemade Gumdrops	173
Ice Box Cookies	159
Lemony Raisin Bars	165
Luscious Carrot Cookies	156
Marble Squares	167
Mattie Cookies (Butterscotch)	157

Molasses Crinkles 158
Molasses Raisin Cookies 157
Monster Bars 167
Oatmeal Cookies 159
Oatmeal Cranberry White
   Chocolate Cookies 159
Peaches N' Cream Bars 168
Peanut Butter Dream Bars 169
Peanut Butter S'mores 174
Pumpkin Pie Squares 170
Reese's Pieces Bars 170
Sour Cream Raisin Bars 171
Strawberry Cream Cookies 160
Tri-Level Brownies 172
Ultimate Chocolate Chip Cookie
   and Fudge Brownie Bar 163
Vermont Maple Cookies 160
White Chocolate Snickerdoodles ... 161

Desserts

Apple Strudel 177
Butter Pecan Sauce 188
Butterscotch Sauce 179
Caramel Dumplings 177
Caramel Pudding 178
Caramel Topping for Ice Cream 188
Chocolate Lasagna 178
Chocolate Topping for Ice Cream ... 188
Creamy Fruit Tapioca 178
Dairy Queen Ice Cream 187
Date Pudding 179
Flan 180
Frozen Mocha Torte 180
Fruit Pizza 181
Homemade Ice Cream 187
Ice Cream Topping 188
Lemon Chiffon Pudding 181
Mocha Dessert 182
Oreo Ice Cream Dessert 182
Pumpkin Pie Squares 182
Pumpkin Torte 183
Quickie Brownie Sundaes 186
Reese's Pudding 184
Rhubarb Danish 184
Strawberry Brownie Trifle 184
Strawberry Ice Cream 187
Tapioca Pudding 185
Tiramisu Cheesecake Dessert 185
Toffee Coffee Dessert 186

Pies

Apple Cranberry Pie 192
Apple Crumb Pie 193
Easy Peach Cream Pie 194
Graham Cracker Crumb Crust 191
Key Lime Pie 193
Peach Cream Pie 194
Pecan Pie 194
Pie Crusts 191
Pumpkin Pie 195
Raisin Creme Pie 195
Raisin Crumb Pie 196
Southern Coconut Pie 196
Strawberry Pie 197
Strawberry Pie Filling Mix 197
Vanilla Crumb Pie Filling 197

Canning, Freezing

Apple Pie Filling 201
Blackberry Jam 201
Canned Apple Pie Filling 201
Canned Deer Chunks 209
Cheese Sauce 209
Deer Meat to Can 208
Dilly Beans 202
Fig Jam 202
Freezer Cucumber Salad 204
Frozen Strawberry Jam 202
Ketchup 205
Pickled Okra 203
Pickled Okra 203
Pizza Sauce 206
Pizza Sauce 206
Port Clinton Pickles 203
Sauerkraut 205
Sweet Dill Slices 204
Tomato Soup 208
V-8 Juice 207
V-8 Tomato Juice 207

Miscellaneous

Amish Mixed Peanut Butter 213
Boiled Peanuts 213
Cinnamon Butter 213
Cold Remedy 213
Cough Syrup 213
Homemade Play Dough 214
Preserving Children 214
Tupperware and Stainless
   Steel Cleaner 214